# THERE I GO
# AGAIN

# THERE I GO AGAIN

## HOW TO KEEP FROM FALLING FOR THE SAME OLD SIN

### Steven Mosley

WORD PUBLISHING
Dallas·London·Vancouver·Melbourne

**There I Go Again**
Copyright © 1991 Steven Mosley

Unless otherwise indicated, Scripture quotations are from the Holy Bible, New International Version (NIV). Copyright © 1973, 1978, 1984 International Bible Society. Used by permission of Zondervan Bible Publishers.

Scripture quotations marked AMP are from the Amplified Bible. Copyright © 1965 Zondervan Publishing House. Used by permission.

Scripture quotations marked NASB are from the New American Standard Bible, © The Lockman Foundation 1960, 1962, 1963, 1968, 1971, 1973, 1975, 1977.

Scripture quotations marked NEB are from the New English Bible. Copyright © the Delegates of the Oxford University Press and the Syndics of the Cambridge University Press, 1961, 1970. Reprinted by permission.

Scripture quotations marked RSV are from the Revised Standard Version of the Bible, copyrighted 1946, 1952, © 1971, 1973 by the Division of Christian Education of the National Council of the Churches of Christ in the U.S.A., and used by permission.

Illustrations by Craig Simmons.

**Library of Congress Cataloging-in-Publication Data**
Mosley, Steven R., 1952–
There I go again: how to keep from falling for the same old sin / by
    Steven Mosley.
        p.   cm.
    ISBN 0-8499-3270-X
    1. Sin. 2. Sins. 3. Temptation. 4. Christian life — 1960–
I. Title.
BV4625.M586 1991
241'.3 — dc20                                      91-8665
                                                      CIP

1 2 3 9 AGF 9 8 7 6 5 4 3 2 1
*Printed in the United States of America*

# Contents

# Introduction
# Rewriting Our Minds

I LOVE the feel of grass and dirt under my cleats, the heat of my limbs churning as fast as they can, and the occasional thrill of intercepting the arching flight of a football under an open sky. And so every fall I drive over to a local Christian high school, strap on yellow flags, slip into a green net jersey, and join the kids in their intramural season of six-man flag football.

Okay, I love competing, too. So far I've been able to hush up the inevitable protests of my middle-aged body enough to keep up with these teenage semi-jocks. Getting out on the field is still a rush for me. And it's great to go all out against another team and still retain a sense of camaraderie and mutual respect.

But it doesn't always work that way. Sometimes, in fact, the games have been something of a disaster. I recall one in particular, toward the end of the season when we were playing the team quarterbacked by Jerry, the high school Bible teacher. They were number one and we were right behind them.

After we'd exchanged several touchdowns, things started heating up in several ways. Jerry's complaints about the referee's calls intensified. Our team captain, the P.E. teacher, began arguing back. Then more and more of us started yelling about almost every play. Hey, that was an illegal block! He was guarding the flag! He almost tackled me! That was roughing the passer!

Jerry, who was something of an authority on flag football rules, was getting more and more upset about the officiating. They just weren't getting it right. The P.E. teacher continued protesting back at him. Soon we were arguing and yelling more than playing the game. Things got mean. One of my teammates, another church member who'd volunteered to play, burst out with a stream of pretty vicious expletives after ripping off Jerry's flags in the backfield. He was looking for blood.

Then Jerry just came apart. He refused to play any more until the referees got their act together. He continued haranguing them for about fifteen minutes while the rest of us sat uncomfortably in a huddle. As I looked around at the faces of those high school kids, the disaster began to sink in.

It was the adult Christian leaders who were doing most of the yelling. The kids just wanted to play, but the teachers had fallen into a protracted confrontation. I had been part of the problem, too, not always keeping my mouth shut when I should have. Worst of all, it was the Bible teacher who'd come unglued and went on and on making a scene in front of the same kids who had listened to him talk quite persuasively in class about the advantages of the Christian life.

What were these teenagers to think? They had heard all about "growth in grace" and "new life in Christ" and "transformed from glory to glory." The right words had been poured into most of them since kindergarten. But now, as they looked at people who had had years to mature and make the Christian life real, it all dissolved under pressure. Unfortunately, this wasn't an isolated incident. I've seen the ugly melodrama repeated in basketball and baseball season, too—Bible-believing, Jesus-loving teachers behaving in exactly the same way as those hot-tempered pagan jocks on television.

After such incidents, we *might* be able to persuade those kids that Jesus can give some kind of ephemeral peace and joy which shows up in church or at spiritual retreats. But it would be a hard sell to make them believe that the Lord can change habits, chronic problems.

## The Same Old Sin

Why is it that Christians in general don't seem to stand out very well from the general population in terms of observable moral behavior? Various polls and surveys have failed to uncover any significant statistical differences between how Christians and non-Christians act on a day-to-day basis. We can certainly hope that the polls are flawed and point out that self-reporting is not a terribly accurate way to measure moral behavior. But still, the fact that Christ doesn't make a more obvious difference in our lives is rather disturbing.

The scandal of Christianity is that so few of us change significantly. Believers talk about "growing in Christ" as one of the givens of the faith. To be in a healthy relationship with Jesus means that we're progressing in that relationship. It's easy to say the right words. Yes, we are growing closer to Jesus every day. Yet when we stop and take a hard look at what exactly is changing inside us, evidence is usually hard to come by.

We can simulate growth with occasional moments of devotion and spurts of resolve, but year after year, we keep falling for the same old sins. We're still entangled in the same old habits and bent out of shape by the same old weaknesses. Veteran Christian counselor Jay E. Adams gives an example of the lament he hears most frequently: "I do fine for a couple of weeks, but the first thing you know, there I go again, battling the same old habits and sins. It's like climbing the mountain and reaching the top, only to find myself at the bottom having to climb it all over again." What has really happened to us in our years of "Christian living"? That can be a very disturbing question.

## Our Life Challenge

Our genes, our upbringing, and our choices have left us with certain soft spots which the flesh, the world, and the devil naturally exploit. We all have these areas of weakness where temptation comes knocking over and over again. Too often those soft spots turn into blind spots. We go on maneuvering around the problem, building our layers of defense—not between ourselves and sin but between ourselves and conviction.

But if we take seriously those old phrases about "growing in Christ" and "new life in the Spirit," we have to confront those sins that go to the core. We have to deal with what our personalities make us prone to do or not do. That's our life challenge: managing a weakness, replacing unhealthy habits, overcoming chronic sin, substituting God's strength for our vulnerability. We have to go beyond the peripheral adjustments, such as arranging a few details of our life in a more religious way. We must go beyond temporary efforts that buckle under and send us back to square one every time the wind picks up.

The Bible illuminates and promotes hard-core change. It does not, however, advertise a quick fix: "Ten days and a couple of follow-ups and you're cured." Scripture presents our problem in its starkest terms: "Can the Ethiopian change his skin or the leopard his spots? Neither can you do good who are accustomed to doing evil" ( Jeremiah 13:23).

Jeremiah's rhetorical question gives poetic force to the revealing confession of Paul in Romans 7: "For what I do is not the good I want to do; no, the evil I do not want to do—this I keep on doing" (v.19).

But the grim realism of Scripture is always followed by bright hopes and extravagant promises. We are assured that we can become new creatures in Christ, that we can actually partake of the divine nature, that the "law of the spirit of life in Christ" can set us free from the "law of sin and death." Surely this involves our deepest habits, the sins that just won't let us go.

## Writing In Our Minds

So how does it happen? Scientists in recent years have made fascinating discoveries about how the brain works, which throw some light on the problem. We've learned that in the dense, convoluted circuitry of our grey matter, electro-chemical pathways are laid out which are the basis of habit formation.

Each of the billions of neurons (nerve cells) in our brain has tens of thousands of connections with other neurons. Between the sending and receiving fibers of these cells is the tiny, all-important space called the *synaptic cleft*. That's where message sent must jump across and become message received.

Various chemicals, called *neurotransmitters*, are what close the gap; that is, they stimulate the fibers to send the message down the nerve line. These chemicals are secreted by tiny button-like enlargements, called *boutons*, on the sending fiber. According to Dr. Elden Chalmers of Loma Linda University, "We've discovered, with powerful microscopes, that some sending fibers have many boutons, while others have only a few. And the sending fibers with many boutons required less stimulation to secrete those message-sending chemicals. We've also found that repeated stimulation does cause boutons to enlarge and multiply. So, we can assume, that any thought or action which is repeated often actually builds little boutons on the end of nerve fibers. And that makes it easier to repeat the same thought or action the next time."

But communication in the brain, like communication between people with brains, is not a simple one-way process. The receiving cell also affects the process — by the state of a chemical structure called the *neuroreceptor*. The neuroreceptor can stimulate, inhibit, or facilitate the message sent across by neurotransmitters. Dr. Gerald May, author of *Addiction and Grace*, likens this feedback to various responses people give each other in conversation, like "I can't hear you," or "Whoa, slow down," or "Please go on."

This gives us some idea of how habits are actually formed neurologically. First we have a message repeated. Cell A starts firing away. Then we have the response. The more we react positively to the message or impulse, the more our neuroreceptors are structured to say, "Please go on." The impulse fires through all the more strongly. Thoughts and words and actions which are sent and responded to over and over actually become a permanent part of the brain; they're written down in terms of electrochemical changes.

UCLA Professor of Psychiatry Dr. Deane Wolcott sees these bouton changes as "one good example of a very complicated business. What we do know is that well-supported patterns of electrical activity result in enduring changes in the structure of the brain."

This is what is meant by "pathways" established through our central nervous system. It's like grooves worn deeper and deeper in our minds. Our thoughts and behaviors can be likened to water flowing through those channels. Water will tend to flow through whatever groove is deepest. We have all established a network of grooves — thought and behavior patterns — which we naturally follow.

**Burning Out**

So what about changing those thought and behavior patterns? Why is it so difficult? One important reason is that we usually try to overcome habits on the receiving end of the electrochemical process. Here's the problem: Most of the ways we resist temptation actually reinforce temptation. Resisting a message is really just another way of responding to it. If the reaction against it is strong, the message will usually keep firing strongly. We're paying attention to the message, so it keeps coming.

Think of it this way. When you turn on the air-conditioner in your living room, you will hear its noise for a while as the whir of its motor registers in your mind. But when you turn your attention to some specific task, you cease to really hear the noise. It's as if the volume were turned way down; it's in the background. That's because your mind generally pays attention to only one thing at a time. Your concentration on the task at hand shuts out irrelevant stimuli.

But let's say you sit down in that room with the air conditioner on and try to make yourself not pay attention to the noise. You keep saying, "Don't listen to it; don't think about it." It will be extremely hard to do so; the noise of the air conditioner, of course, will remain the center of attention.

It's even harder to do this when the noise is some nice, juicy temptation. The more we "resist" it, the more it dominates our attention. That's why we can pray at length in great earnestness about some besetting sin and then turn around and fall right back into it. Our intense reaction to the temptation keeps the message firing strongly.

Now it is possible to continue saying no to this noise and build up a barrier against it. Through practice we can keep building up those inhibitor neuroreceptors: "Pipe down for pity's sake. Please!" And if we are persistent enough, we can usually block out the message.

But it's still there, the channel has been dug, the water has flowed. We can build a dam, and hope to keep that flow interrupted. But any disturbance, like an emotional letdown or a period of stress, will usually break the dam. And suddenly we find ourselves right back in the habit again. We marvel that it is still so strong; we thought we'd overcome it a long time ago. In our neural network, breaking pathways are the first to fail under stress; they go down before action pathways do. In other words, it takes more energy, more electrochemical firing, to say "Hold it" than "Go ahead."

The big problem with habits is always relapse. The message keeps breaking through our defenses. Most of us simply can't sustain a protracted battle with sin. We can't keep on putting out those inhibitory neuroreceptors to the message that keeps firing intensely. Having to always stand on guard, keeping an ear out for that noise, that juicy temptation—which will surely come by again—wears us down. We will eventually burn out on this kind of struggle to be good.

## Rewriting with the Word

Work on the receiving end is valid; there are times when we need to tell unhealthy messages to shut up. But I suggest that another strategy is more important for long-term success, something much more healthy and sustainable. And that is simply making *alternative pathways*. We deliberately bring in substitute messages and respond to them positively. In neurological terms, we build up the boutons on other axons, stimulate other facilitating neuroreceptors. In behavioral terms, we turn our attention to another task, an alternative track, and allow the temptation to become background noise. We build a deeper groove for the substitute message than the rut of our chronic sin.

In other words, *we rewrite our minds*.

I believe this is what Scripture aims at when it informs us that we are transformed by the "renewing of our minds." This is presented as the alternative to imitating the pattern of the world. It's not just blocking the temptation, telling carnal messages to pipe down. It's renewing our minds, putting in something new, rewriting. It all relates to the new covenant, to our privilege, as believers in Christ, of having his Spirit work inside us.

Jeremiah quoted Jehovah as presenting his new covenant in these terms: "I will put my law in their minds and write it on their hearts" ( Jeremiah 31:33). The new heart of the new covenant involves rewriting — with the Word of God. The creative Word is to abide in us richly and fruitfully. This book is about how that rewriting takes place.

## From Piano to Saxophone

It's obvious from our glaring failure to deal with chronic sin that we all need practice in rewriting. When a person first sits down to learn to play the piano, she will at first move her fingers over the keys very slowly as she attempts to find the right one to go with the right dot in her music book. Messages must find the right pathways through her brain, make the right connections. But slowly as she repeats this process, the messages fire through more quickly, the pathways are established. Soon certain finger movements become automatic; she doesn't have to consciously go through all the steps from this series of notes to that chord structure on the keys. It just happens. Her brain is "wired" for piano playing; the necessary messages are written in her mind.

When we confront a habit or some chronic sin, we are dealing with writing in our brains. A series of thoughts and responses, like those involved in piano playing, is programmed in. We can do it all without thinking; it feels natural. Changing a habit, on the other hand, is like learning to play another instrument, say a saxophone. We have to learn to react to those notes in different ways; our fingers move slowly and clumsily over the apertures on the new instrument; our brains must gradually re-circuit and make the right connections. It's not easy. That's why we go back to the piano so often.

And that's why we relapse into habits so often. With moral behavior, the fact that the old habit is usually much more appealing on the surface doesn't help matters. While we're fiddling around with the new instrument, those other established patterns are telling us to race back to the familiar keys.

But we *can* learn to play the saxophone — especially if we focus our attention on it and stop staring at the piano. And those first few sweet notes that we manage to coax out of it will encourage us to make many more. The same processes that work to establish unhealthy habits can work to establish healthy ones.

**Sustainable Change**

That's what we want to learn about. Rewriting our minds, becoming inspired with a new skill instead of just trying to eradicate an old compulsion. Everything I'm suggesting in these chapters is aimed toward that end: turning a weary struggle into a good fight, turning spurts of resistance into something positive and sustainable. Too often I've heard sincere believers say: "I've tried so hard for so long, yet I still fail in the same old ways." I get the feeling that too many people have come up empty after investing so much in the struggle to overcome sin. That's tragic.

I believe there's a way to invest ourselves that will leave us full at the end. There's a way to fashion our fight into something spiritually stimulating instead of spiritually exhausting. There's a way to accept the challenge of growth over the long haul that builds us up instead of burns us out. We can gain experiences with eternal value *in the fight itself,* no matter what our level of success at the moment. We may always have a tendency to stray in a particular direction, but that tendency can be turned on its head and made a stimulus for life-changing encounters with Christ.

## Getting Down to Ground Level

In my own long battles, I've been frustrated with many of the "Christian answers" typically given for the problem of growth. What should I do? Fall on the Rock? Let go and let God? Persevere in faith? Reach out my hand to the Man? Overcome by the Spirit?

I recognize that there must be some important truth behind such phrases, but what is it exactly? It can all seem so spiritually intangible. Some people try to get beyond the clichés and be helpful. We hear advice like: "Falling on the Rock means that you place your will in the hands of God." "Persevering in faith signifies that you continue to trust Christ to see you through a difficulty." "Overcoming by the Spirit means we appropriate the Spirit's inner power to deal with sin."

This is a little better, but too often we just have one set of clichés replaced by another. Talk about reaching out becomes talk about appropriating; mortification becomes submission; persevering in faith is revamped as continuing to trust.

Admittedly, it's hard for all of us to really put a finger on the nuts-and-bolts of change in the Christian life. It's not something we can measure under a microscope or quantify in some formula. Human life is always more rich and complex than its labels; divine life much more so. That's one reason we're stuck so often with phrases pointing vaguely in this or that direction.

But it's not the whole reason. Another factor is simply our failure to dig deeply enough. We throw slogans at change and hope for the best, more than tackle the problem experimentally. As Goethe once wrote, "When an idea is wanting, a word can always be found to take its place." But in the dust and sweat of real struggle with sin and virtue, the labels do tend to break down into tangible components. You do get a finger on something concrete — on what you can do specifically.

So in this book we'll try to get behind all the phrases to the most specific point possible. We need to get to ground level: the doable.

In preparing this book I've considered what godly men and women down through the ages have had to say about specific change, but the chapters that follow are really more like notes scribbled from the front lines in the heat of battle. They are tips that veterans might pass along to each other while new recruits listen in. I've tried to whittle down the counsel to simply what works and what doesn't: this strategy has kept me going; that biblical practice has wrested victory from the jaws of defeat. It's based on moments of despair, hours of frustration, and times of great joy when I stumbled into principles that have helped me deal with a deeply-imbedded habit and, yes, grow.

# 1

# An Honest Agreement

THERE was a time when Julia dutifully confessed her outbursts to the Lord with a great deal of feeling. She hated to hurt those closest to her and so prayed earnestly that she might stop her habit of venting anger on the kids when things upset her. She tried to continue confessing this sin whenever she caught herself falling into the old pattern of verbal abuse. Her daughter was very sensitive and could be deeply wounded by cutting words. Her son was growing more and more sullen. After seeing a certain Walt Disney movie, he began mumbling a new retort to Mommy's outbursts: "Old Yeller."

Julia wanted to change, but there were so many days which brought an overload of stress: working part-time in a hectic office, rushing to get the kids from school, trying to deal with their minor tragedies and major quarrels, cleaning up after everyone's messes—it was just too much. Time after time she found herself blowing up at the kids over little accidents or indiscretions. And after a while she began just whispering a quick prayer—still rather earnest, but no big pause in her schedule; she regretted the incident and went on about her business. Slowly Julia's response to her habit, which did not diminish, became more and more a thought or two, and less and less a genuine prayer. After blowing up, she'd slip into a kind of auto-confession mode: "Whoops, sorry about that." She'd chide herself for screaming and leave it at that.

One evening, after months of this auto-confession, Julia recalled that she'd hardly paused after unloading on her daughter that day. She realized with a start that her confession to God had faded out altogether, becoming simply a moment of calm after the storm, an empty set. Her periodic outbursts were continuing, unbroken by any conscious confession or repentance. In the back of her mind she still saw this as sinful, but in practice, nothing was happening to indicate that. Almost by default, verbal abuse had become an accepted practice in her life.

Ernie had done it again. How could he? He'd fantasized about that gorgeous coed walking down the sidewalk and now stood accused as shameless adulterer. Time to confess again. Back in his room he knelt down and poured out his bitter disappointment. Why did he keep falling into this same pattern of lust? He was a miserable wretch full of every kind of foul desire; he'd offended the holy God over and over.

Ernie sincerely tried to make himself hate the sin that kept tripping him up. Lust was demonic, nothing but cheap exploitation, a defiler of the soul. He just had to get it out of his life. Ernie pleaded with God for forgiveness and asked to be made to loathe the terrible sin that haunted him.

Back out on the campus, he felt so miserable for a while that he couldn't look at anyone. He knew that transgression threatened him everywhere. And then, incredibly enough, just as he was reminding himself to abhor lust, he slipped into it again. Eyeing another attractive girl and thinking about how awful lust is, he began paying homage to it. Adulterous fantasy swept him up once more. Wretched, wretched thoughts! Time to confess again. So Ernie trudged back to his room to try once more to become *really* aware of the evil that had made him fall.

Julia and Ernie show us two ways in which an unhealthy kind of confession actually aids and abets an unhealthy habit. If biblical confession is to be a great wall of defense around us, these two people certainly fell off it, and they fell in opposite directions. One didn't confess enough and ended up subconsciously capitulating to a familiar sin. The other appeared to confess too much and fell into an obsessive pattern that only made him more vulnerable to his habit. When it comes to bad habits and confession, sometimes it seems as if we're hooked if we do and hooked if we don't.

## Agreement, Not Persuasion

To get a healthy grip on confession, let's first take a look at what it is—and what it isn't. People often approach this Christian duty as a task of persuading God to bestow forgiveness. They give reasons, excuses, present their frailty, explain how sorry they are, and hope that the divine will is thus nudged toward pardon. The feeling is that one must create forgiveness out of nothing. It doesn't exist yet, but our earnest petition may bring it into being—changing wrath into mercy and a debit in the divine ledger into a credit.

This attitude places too much weight on our act of confession and repentance. We must avoid turning confession into some kind of mini-atonement where we try to make up for our wrong before God and be so utterly nice and pious that He can't help but bestow grace. The fact is, all the really hard work has already been done. Forgiveness, pardon, and justification have been chiseled out for us through Christ's blood, sweat, and tears. Slain on the cross as the spotless Lamb, Christ took on transgressions and created forgiveness out of nothing. It does not exist apart from Christ's sacrificial act.

So confession is not talking God into something; it's not a sales job. That would be like trying to persuade Michelangelo to repaint the Sistine Chapel ceiling every time we walk in and look up at those glorious scenes. We have to first believe that the masterpiece is finished; nothing can be added to the forgiveness that the spotless Lamb has already laid out for us in the larger-than-life scene of Golgotha. What we must do is claim it as a great vault of spectacular mercy which covers us right now, as we are, with this messy sin all over our hands.

The Greek word used in the New Testament for confession has a root meaning of assent, agreement. We agree with God in confession: *Yes, I have sinned; this is wrong; I claim Your costly pardon; thank You for lavishing Your forgiveness on me right now.* As heart-felt agreement with God, confession can become a healthy way to take the first definite step away from a chronic sin.

## Who We Confess To

Keeping in mind exactly who is receiving our confession also makes a big difference. A God who cherishes us is listening intently. He is the One quite eager to throw our transgressions into the chasms of the sea. There is nothing in the universe which can separate us from His lovingkindness. No one else sees more deeply into our pernicious habits, and no one else believes in us so passionately. We make good confession to fulfill God's love, not appease His anger.

Keeping the face of God in mind as we confess will help us open up more easily and more honestly in prayer. The Father whose love is higher than the heavens is also the Lord who sees into our innermost being. Nothing is hidden from His sight.

Habits normally create a sophisticated array of defenses in order to survive on the same turf as our conscience. Our mental circuitry is well-programmed with excuses. For the obese, today's hefty slab of fudge cake is always a preamble to tomorrow's diet. The hothead who has kicked a hole in the door again says his defenses are down due to a touch of the flu. The chronic complainer maintains that she can't possibly be cheerful after listening to the world's problems on the morning news.

Because religious people are particularly vulnerable to guilt, their bad habits require a host of allies, ways to rationalize, play sleight-of-habit, and pretend the problem is not really there. The longer a habit persists, the more our minds become a Gothic edifice full of hidden passageways and trap doors where we can ignore the obvious and postpone the inevitable.

Most common of all is our tendency to see the habit as something separate from ourselves. It's this monkey on my back, this foreign object lodged in my system.

While conducting a test one day in my high school Spanish class I had an unexpected visitor. A student named Ted burst through the door and glanced around the classroom with fire in his eyes. As I protested that we were having an exam, he spotted his prey, walked over to the back row where a kid named Gary was seated, yelled at him, and punched him in the face.

At that point I saw red, too, and quickly propelled the intruder out the door, down the hall and into the principal's office, dumped him in a chair, and yelled at him. After class we all got together, and I discovered that Gary had smeared eggs on Ted's car. Ted apologized to me meekly, saying, "I didn't know what I was doing." I accepted his apology, of course, and also said I regretted losing my temper.

Later, what struck me most was Ted's almost reflexive reasoning: "I didn't know what I was doing." The pressure of the moment, you see, temporary insanity. It seemed the appropriate thing to say at the time. But the boy knew exactly what he was doing; he'd walked all over the school in search of Gary, his anger building by the second. He'd probably given my student a real pounding over and over in his mind before finally confronting him in class.

As it happened, this young man had a bad temper which exploded on other occasions, too. Reflecting on him after graduation I wondered if he ever owned that anger, or if it always remained something separate — "not really me."

Confession is our way of saying finally, "It's me. I own the problem." We step out of our Gothic edifice; we drop whatever defenses we've been using and expose ourselves to the all-seeing God.

Though confession is the essential first step in dealing with sinful behavior, we should keep in mind that all habit is not sin. We certainly shouldn't regard feelings of depression, for example, as sinful, though they may sometimes lead us to wrongdoing. And feelings of anger do not necessarily involve acts of transgression. So in some cases our "honest agreement" with God need be only that we have a problem and require His help. Whatever our difficulty, open and sincere communication with the One who knows and loves us is still our starting point. However, since the majority of the habits that plague us involve sinful attitudes and actions, this chapter concentrates on confession as an admission of guilt.

**Where We Confess**

God has provided a special place where confession can take healthy shape. It is the Hebrew temple of the Old Testament, the holy ground where God's people were instructed to take their sins. It's a place that still speaks to us today through its symbols and helps us avoid the pitfalls of Julia and Ernie. That's where we first meet the act of confession in Scripture, and that's where it is most graphically symbolized.

Picture a man named Eleaz walking through the encampment of Israel under a burning Palestinian sky. The sharp shadows of neighbors mending tents and grinding barley fall across his path as he leads a perfect white lamb toward the smoke of the sanctuary. Most look away politely. A transgression against the law of Jehovah has moved Eleaz to select this young animal without blemish from his small flock.

Arriving at the temple enclosure, Eleaz, the guilty party, waits with bleating lamb for a priest to assist him. He fingers the edge of his knife and then, at a signal, walks over to the large stone altar of burnt sacrifice. The innocent victim trots along at his side. A priest directs Eleaz to place his hand on the head of the lamb—his guilt is now acknowledged and transferred to the spotless one. At this point Eleaz confesses his sin silently to God. And then he quickly reaches around to the lamb's throat, feels for a vein, and slits it open.

Blood flows copiously; death comes quickly. The priest catches the dark liquid in a large bowl and sprinkles it on the horns at the four corners of the altar. Then he places the carcass on the altar and burns it.

## The Beauty of Sacrifice

Confession in the Hebrew temple first of all proclaimed sacrifice. The deadly nature of sin could not have been more strongly embodied than at the moment when the prize lamb of Eleaz's herd jerked, kicked, and went limp in his hands. Sin is costly. Innocent life-blood spilled on the ground. A kind of life-saving surgery happened there where an infirmity from one was transplanted to another.

But there was more, too. All the symbols in that temple focused on cleansing, on purity. Once the animal had been slain, everything echoed the major theme: forgiveness. The smoke wafting up from that body was described as a sweet-smelling aroma to the Lord. Yahweh wasn't squinting down at the ugliness of Eleaz's sin; He was looking at the beauty of pure sacrifice on the man's behalf.

The shed blood itself, contrary to our impressions, symbolized life; it cleansed. Blood did not pollute; it purified. Just past the altar stood a laver where the priest washed his hands, another emblem of cleansing. Beyond that, a curtained entrance led into the holy place of the temple itself. Here a candelabra, a table of shewbread, and an altar of incense sent up sacred light, bread of life, and a holy fragrance to the holy God. Finally, in the inner sanctum, the Most Holy Place, a mercy seat covering the ark of the covenant made God's throne an epicenter of forgiveness. Everything in the temple, from the priest's garments to the cherubim woven into the temple drapes, reverberated the central idea of purity.

The sanctuary is valuable as a visual clue that can move us from temptation or sin to an appreciation of grace. We don't have to meditate on all the details of the Hebrew temple every time we fall. But it can vividly suggest a definite place in which to turn from sin. Visible scenes are more quickly imprinted in our minds than abstractions. The sin that besets us is almost always something specific; it's there where we can see it. It can be scripted into our minds with relative ease. Non-sin, however, is not there. It's more of an abstraction. That's why it's useful to have a concrete, visual clue that we can write in as a detour around sin or guilt. We don't want to keep looking (angrily) at that sin and therefore keep reinforcing it. Instead, we can remember the temple and allow it to fire off a series of associations about forgiveness. That sanctuary cues us into rewriting a healthy confession script in our minds.

## The Sorrow That Leads to Life

Many people remember exactly where they were when they heard the news John F. Kennedy had been shot, or the news of the space shuttle Challenger blowing up. I remember another piece of news that froze all the details of life around me unforgettably. I was at my desk, glancing at the coldly random letters in a white computer keyboard, surrounded by bare beige walls, with the sound of my children's voices filtering in from outside, my body suddenly buzzing, the books on my shelf staring back dully. A surgeon was telling me over the phone that the lump he'd just removed from my wife's breast was malignant. I remember the question looming over that moment—what is the rest of our lives going to be like?

I was calm, but something irrevocable had happened, like a war declared in some far-off, obscure country which may quickly sweep over you. At the hospital I watched Kaz slowly emerge from the anesthetic, fumbling with a piece of knowledge; the doctor had told her something. And standing by those horribly white sheets, looking at her pale face with features not altogether composed yet, I had to confirm the bad news.

## A Beeline to the Physician

The Bible presents sin as a deadly malignancy that we must deal with squarely. Isaiah, for example, grabs us by the throat and presents a frightening spectre of a diagnosis:
"From the sole of your foot to the top of your head
　　there is no soundness —
only wounds and welts
　　and open sores,
not cleansed or bandaged
　　or soothed with oil" (Isaiah 1:6).
This picture of raw, open wounds shouts urgency, trauma, a desperate need for healing. No casual bandaid or banal word of comfort will do; this is a matter of life and death.

Confession accepts the seriousness of sin. It sorrows. But as Paul pointed out, there's good sorrow and bad sorrow. He distinguished between "godly sorrow," which leads to salvation, and "worldly sorrow," which leads to death. It's possible, for example, to simply worry ourselves to death about a malignancy. If we see no real way of combating the disease or if we spend our time thinking about all the cancer cells that must be coursing through us, our sorrow simply speeds up the deadly process. However, if there is a physician with an effective remedy nearby, and our sorrow over the shocking bad news makes us rush off to see that doctor, then our sorrow has led to our rescue.

I remember visiting the surgeon with Kaz so he could deliver the verdict on further treatment and its chances of success. We walked into his office under a withering load of fear. All the healthy people walking by apparently without a care seemed like aliens from another planet. I thought, *If only, if only that tumor could have been somewhere else.*

The good news is that with the malignancy of sin, the impossible hope does come true. We come into the office of our Physician and hear an incredible announcement: The tumor is indeed elsewhere—in Christ crucified.

Confession needs to be a very serious beeline to our skillful Physician for forgiveness. It must never be a mechanical, perfunctory transaction—like handing the pharmacist a prescription for some pills. No, this is more serious. Surgery was required; blood had to flow; the body of Christ was violated in order that sin might not destroy us.

## Which Picture We Carry

So we come back to the Julia and Ernie dilemma, apparently confessing too little and too much. Julia had better ask herself if she has ever really sorrowed about this particular problem. It's no longer a malignancy to her, but more like a mosquito bite that she attempts to swat away—always too late, you can't swat away the bite, of course, only the mosquito. Julia gradually stopped returning the Doctor's calls. She needs a good visit with that Physician in order to acknowledge the seriousness of her problem, own it, lay claim to the Healer's sacrifice, and then go on as a woman thankful for forgiveness.

Ernie, on the other hand, tried to cure himself by staring long and hard at that nasty tumor. He needs to move from the spectre of sin to a concentration on the cure. He is forgiven; that fact must become bigger in his mind than the threat of sin. But he keeps losing sight of the remedy because of his agonized appraisal of the malignancy. He has lost a sense of the strategic value of sorrow because he is constantly returning to square one. He has forgotten that Jesus asked us, after fasting and mourning over sin, to wash our faces and go outside with a big smile.

Healthy grief is a process; it should lead us somewhere. As Paul advised, godly sorrow should lead us to repentance and salvation. Julia was not sorrowing, and Ernie was treating sorrow as an end in itself, getting stuck in the first stages of the grieving process. The problem for both of them was not simply confessing too little or too much; it was neglecting to find the kind of sorrow that leads to life.

Good confession involves a good, hard look at the malignancy, acknowledging it with sorrow, and then a good hard turning away from it (repentance). We don't carry a picture of the tumor around with us; we carry a picture of the Great Physician. As D. L. Moody put it, "The voice of sin may be loud, but the voice of forgiveness is louder."

## Counting on Confession

Julia and Ernie represent two extremes in relating to sin. Both failed to experience the kind of sorrow that leads to life. Others of us maintain a relatively good hold on healthy confession, but still manage to misuse it at times. In fact, repentance itself can be used as an excuse to sin.

I once found myself taking advantage of God's ever-ready forgiveness, counting on His mercy even as I entered into a habitual sin. It related to my old nemesis: pornography. I realized I was in big trouble when one of my excuses for sneaking off with a magazine or video was my assurance that, after all, I would be repenting so soon and so earnestly that all would be well in the end. As I was praying and reading Scripture in the aftermath, trying to get some genuine repentance just after I had used genuine repentance as a pretext for sin, I hit on a picture of what I'd been doing.

Let's say you go into a bar with your good buddy who has been trying desperately to get you to stop drinking. You ignore his pleading, saunter up to the counter, and ask for a shot of whiskey. Now imagine that your buddy has told the bartender to punch him in the face every time you take a drink. He's that desperate on your behalf. You take a big swig and *pow*, the brawny bartender sends your buddy flying off his stool. You're not inconsiderate; you gently pick your friend off the floor, dust him off, and sit him back up on the stool beside you. But then, with itchy fingers slipping around the glass, you quickly down another shot.

Another fist to the face. Again you very solicitously pick your friend up, adjust his jacket, dab at the side of his mouth with your handkerchief—and then ask the bartender to pour you another. *Smack!* This ritual continues until you're pretty oblivious to the pain—and keep jawing in a very neighborly way with your good buddy, talking about how much he means to you and wiping his bloody face with your handkerchief.

This little story was the way I got a grip on what I'd been doing. My confession was being bled white of any sorrow; it had become an unfeeling presumption on the sacrifice of a friend. So I needed that jolt to get me back into the sorrow that leads to repentance and salvation.

Seeing our relation to Christ's sacrifice in a new way can help keep us from using repentance as an excuse to sin. But some efforts to "really see" the atonement manage to turn it into an oppressive burden.

### Drip, Drip, Drip

A friend of mine remembers very vividly a life-changing story he heard at a college religious retreat. A minister was speaking at length about the need for perfecting our character and about the horrors of transgression against a holy God. The climax of his call to sinlessness came with this illustration: Every time we sin, it's like dripping burning oil on the exposed body of Christ. Our every moral failure tortures His sensitive soul.

My friend couldn't get this scene out of his mind — drip, drip, drip, all his sins, scores of them every day, falling on his Jesus who cried out in agony. So he dropped out of school, went to an institution where the eradication of transgression had been made an official twenty-four-hour-a-day policy, and sank into a debilitating fanaticism.

Certain kinds of sorrow—even of the most earnest, religious variety—can lead to death. How then should we relate to the malignancy of sin and the sacrificial sufferings of Christ? Are my story in the tavern and my friend's story of burning oil really any different?

Let's first ask this: Do our sins hurt Christ? If we consider that Jesus always loves us and longs for our best, we have to answer yes. But He does not hurt in the same way as when He took on our sins at the Place of the Skull. Scripture assures us that this was a once-and-for-all-time experience. And Jesus took on all our transgressions at the cross — past, present, and future. He does not have to somehow take on new burdens as we continue to sin. So we err greatly if we imagine some kind of perpetual atonement that Christ has to go through. Transgressions were expiated and atoned for in full back at Calvary. That includes paid-in-full on an emotional level, too. The atonement had an end.

Back to our two stories. Perhaps they aren't that different in principle. If my scenario at the bar had become a means of agonizing about Christ crucified anew every time I blew it, then I might have sunk into a sorrow without exit. Fortunately, it remained a means of appreciating His forgiveness based on a past act of sacrifice, a means of ceasing to take advantage of that past act. (And I used it at a strategic moment in my struggle, not every time I slipped.) If the preacher talking about burning oil had made it clear that Christ had suffered very acutely at one time for all sin in order to lavish forgiveness on us, then my friend might not have sunk into a sorrow without exit.

The problem behind our counting on confession beforehand is that we cease to value that past, finished event for what it was. We plan our repentance ahead of time — even as we're planning on giving in to sin. But a premeditated, mechanical confession of deliberate sin is a way of despising Christ's sufferings. We have to acknowledge that fact, agree that this transgression is a deadly danger, and ask God to help us turn from it.

What matters is that we relate to Christ's suffering as a completed act that we must work to *value* more, not *agonize* over more. Being more thankful, more appreciative about the cross is the key, not trying to make ourselves miserable about pounding in the spikes in the present.

**Rose in an Iron Fist**

I was retracing my wayward steps one day after a big fall
and began to feel quite miserable about failing again, over and
over again, without putting up much of a fight. Those slick
images of the flesh had overwhelmed me once more; I'd meekly
laid down my contribution to porn at a nearby store. The depression I was feeling could have turned into a sorrow without exit, so I began looking hard for some scriptural hook on
which to hang my faith.

Alone in my apartment, I stared out at the laundry
hanging on a line and thought it looked as ragged and motley
as my attempts at overcoming this sin. The bright sun drying
the clothes did not seem cheery at all, but only threw a harsh
glare on the weeds and unkempt shrubs loitering around my
quarters.

I confessed, of course, and told God how wretched I felt
for deliberately betraying Him. I claimed forgiveness, but
couldn't find it in my heart to enjoy it. I paced about in the
silence of the house, praying, searching for that lost coin of
grace amid my cluttered rooms. Then I began reading about
Christ's experience in Gethsemane. I thought about the cosmic forces arrayed there for a showdown and the meaning of
Christ's agonizing struggle. I was studying a devotional
commentary on the life of Christ when suddenly the author's
remarks opened a window. I saw this colossally burdened
Messiah as if for the first time. He stood at the pivotal point
of history with the fate of humanity hanging in the balance.
He had to make an excruciating choice; the path toward the
torture chamber had a detour . . . would He take it? No, Christ
submitted to the divine plan. In the end, nothing could turn
Him from His mission; He willed to become the propitiation
for a race that had willed to sin.

It was this stubborn will to save that struck me. Christ
extended forgiveness not as a spontaneous gesture that
circumstances might alter. Sometimes we picture forgiveness as someone handing us a rose. Pardon does indeed have

a fragrance, but Christ offers it to us clenched in an iron fist, as a determined act of grace, immovable in mercy. So I had to take it, and take it altogether.

God had given me a revelation, a bright insight shimmering in the midday gloom of my apartment on which I could hang my faith—and then some. It seemed to me at that moment an exceedingly gracious insight. He was still pouring out the goods, even to the old repeater. He hadn't given up by a long shot, but was itching for another fight. And so in this encouragement I could see how eager He was to pardon. Those words about crimson stains bleached white weren't just "as a general rule" in the abstract; they were clear and specific, here and now. God does forgive. He does move us through the grieving process to the good news.

# 2

# The Wedge of Will

You've been following your diet perfectly, right down to the carrots and cottage cheese. But then someone plops a gorgeous piece of cherry pie down in front of you, with a big scoop of almond vanilla ice cream dripping on the flaky crust, and you feel your will-to-thinness melting away to zero.

You heard a powerful sermon on holiness last Sunday and have decided to be nice to that obnoxious office manager at work. But then the same old problem with his pickiness builds to the same old ruined-my-day resentment and your resolution is bowled over in the same old way.

You're sick and tired of being depressed. You determine to be happy this week. But then friends desert you on the weekend; you're sitting home alone again and that gray mist starts seeping in. You try to will yourself to not get gloomy. You reach around for some leverage, but there's nothing tangible there, nothing to grab hold of, only an unwieldy assortment of feelings all headed one way: down.

Any strategy for changing habits eventually comes up against this thing called "will." Unfortunately it's much more often the culprit than the solution. In fact, for most of us, speaking of our willpower is rather like whistling in the dark. We hope that it exists somewhere in the murky depths of our tempted souls. We hope that it shows up before it's too late. But the thing is hard to get a grip on.

What is this "will" that we're supposed to exercise? Is it the psychologist's "conditioning"? Is it the biblical "heart"?

The action of the will is pretty clear when it comes to choosing between two attractive or neutral options; we decide to go route B instead of route A. But when we are called on to exercise our will continually, as in countering the claims of a habit, then the process muddies. Our will seems to dissolve into impulses, emotions, and a skirmish of conflicting thoughts. An essayist once wrote, "Any time you think you have influence, try ordering around someone else's dog." Chronic habits often behave very much like someone else's dog — and our will can seem an all but impotent "influence."

## Who Is Responsible for Change?

But some believers in Christ and His transforming grace wonder how much we should be counting on the strength of our will in the first place — maybe we shouldn't count on it at all. The question most of us run into at some point in our struggles with chronic sin is: Do we change or does God change us? Who's got the ball in this game? Some conclude that it's all up to the One who saves us. Others insist that we carry the primary responsibility.

There are strong biblical models and slogans for each view. Champions of willpower quote Paul's pointed remark about resisting "to the point of shedding blood in your striving against sin." That certainly sounds like an agonized effort of the will. There is also that familiar battle cry about "fighting the good fight of faith." Those majoring in such texts typically complain that Christians are too passive about sanctification.

But others, who insist that we must "let go and let God," point to texts celebrating the fact that we are saved by faith alone, and that we progress in the Christian life not by "works of the law" but by faith and by God's Spirit. In trying not to be saved by works, they are almost afraid to exercise their wills. These people are fond of the spontaneous-growth analogies: Just like a flower naturally developing in sunlight.

And then those believers caught in the middle, running back and forth between the two strategies, keep asking, "If it's so easy, why is it so hard?"

## 100 Percent/100 Percent.

To get a grip on a healthy exercise of the will, it's useful to first figure out where you actually stand in the spectrum between passive faith and bloodstained will. I'd say most of us don't invest a great deal of energy in this area, and quite a few rarely lift a finger against specific sin. Let's be honest. Look at how and where you place your effort each day. It would be enlightening if we had a Will Meter we could attach to our brains and measure the intensity of mental effort. When would the wires heat up?

Have you ever stayed up almost all night studying for a test? Sure. Have you ever stayed up almost all night praying about a spiritual problem? Uh . . . How about pondering the right time to buy a house—interest rates, points, market values? How many hours have you fretted away trying to figure out how to ask for a raise or get a choice assignment? Have you ever agonized over who is going to win the Super Bowl?

Our brains go into high gear, and stay in high gear over time, for a great variety of causes. We invest intense mental effort all the time on behalf of both trivial pursuits and important decisions. And we don't question the effort. We're alive aren't we? Of course those wires are going to heat up on a regular basis.

But when it comes to moral goals, overcoming sin, pursuing virtue, well, we start looking around for overdrive, some way to coast through this. The prospect of investing mental effort in that direction really puts us off. Or we put up a token resistance to our favorite sin, make a gesture, and then tell God, "Hey I tried, the rest is up to You." My guess is that most of us would fall on the low end of the effort scale, toward passive faith. The standing orders in our brain cells are, "If the moral patient collapses, use no heroic measures to resuscitate him."

But there are others, of course, who do invest a great deal of mental effort into being good. They've tried hard and are genuinely frustrated. The more they attempt to stare down some sin, the more entangled in it they become. Moral progress becomes almost an obsession; persistent evil habits become very depressing.

So what's the answer? Both the person who wants God to do it all (or at least 90 percent), and the one who is struggling desperately (with God's help), need a better model to work from. I suggest this: *Growth is 100 percent God's work and 100 percent our work; it's completely a matter of God's ability and will, and completely a matter of our ability and will.*

Effort is not some mutually exclusive territory; we don't carve it up like a pie and ask God to take on 80 percent of the work load if we pitch in 20 percent. God and I have got to be completely together in this. Paul put it very neatly: "I labor, striving according to His power, which mightily works within me." In growing spiritually we're completely involved as human beings — precisely because God is completely involved. We don't hold back a certain amount of effort so that God will have room to work. Our Father is not a God of gaps. He is not a God of matching funds either; He doesn't only put out to the extent that we put out. Sometimes He provides virtually all the funds, if we only have a widow's mite. But we do need to give whatever we have; we must participate.

Listen to Paul elaborate on this 100 percent/100 percent arrangement. He advised the Philippians: "Continue to work out your salvation with fear and trembling, for it is God who works in you to will and to act according to his good purpose" (Phillippians 2:13). The apostle also said of himself: "I worked harder than all of them—yet not I, but the grace of God that was with me" (1 Corinthians 15:10).

Exercising our will is very similar to exercising our faith. The important thing is that we extend whatever we have out to God and begin using it. Whether we exercise an arm knotted with muscles or one thin as a reed, what matters is that we stretch that limb. We must involve our volition in His almighty volition. It's no use complaining about how poorly our will has served us in the past. Choice has got to be there. When suffering from ill health we may blame our diet, but the remedy is not to stop eating. When we've tried and failed, the remedy is not to write off our will. I sympathize with the often-repeated lament: "Just trying to be good doesn't work." That's very true, but I can also testify that *not* trying to be good doesn't work either. Whatever we do involves some kind of trying. The important thing is the way in which we try.

## A Will Against the Odds

So how do we give 100 percent of our will and still claim God's 100 percent? How do we work and still believe in God working in us? Some believers have advised: "Place your will in God's hands—that's the key!" What does that mean? Even if we could get a handle on the will, how could we make such a firm deposit? Calvary provides a clue.

When a condemned Jesus hung exposed on a cross outside the walls of Jerusalem, when He lurched as his lacerated back rubbed against the wood and felt blood drip down into His mouth and rose on spiked feet for a gasp of air—it took a colossal exercise of will to remain suspended there between heaven and earth as the ultimate derelict. He could have ended the ordeal so easily.

Priests were pointing Him out gloatingly as Exhibit A of their case against His claims. All His messianic promises seemed to slink away in the dust and blood at the foot of the cross. Who could possibly believe in Him now? The Father could not. And that was without question the deepest blow.

God had to look on His Son as sin incarnate; He had to treat
Him as an unrepentant, rebellious outcast.

Denied by the people whose covenant faith He had nurtured over millennia, abandoned by the Father who'd been
one with Him for eternity, Jesus had to will Himself up on
that cross. Through the physical jolts racing brainward from
the skewed nerves in His limbs, through the anguish of betrayal by those closest to Him, through the impenetrable
spiritual night of the second death, He remained steadfast,
arms spread out to the guilty world until His last soul-
wrenching cry in hell.

Calvary spreads out for us a spectacle of Jesus' will against
all the odds. It had started in Gethsemane when Christ was
pressed down to the gnarled roots of olive trees by the awful
specter of His Father's wrath. Everything in Him recoiled
violently from the chasm of sin, but He willed Himself into
submission, willed Himself under the agonizing darkness,
willed Himself into the hands of the mob.

During the hurried, semi-legal proceedings before Pilate
and Herod, He willed Himself to be silent before His accusers,
a mute but eloquent Lamb maneuvered toward the slaughter.
Jesus willed Himself to speak only words that would echo redemption. He would not strike back against the crafty lies and
slanderous abuse of His pious adversaries.

Jesus willed His assaulted body through the streets of
Jerusalem; He set His face hard and true toward the Place of
the Skull. He willed Himself onto the wood to be nailed down
and flung up as a humiliated sign for the largely indifferent
world. No one compelled Christ; no human hand could force
Him through the scenes of His passion. Every step was volun-
tary, every act freely chosen.

Sometimes we don't see that fact in our preoccupation
with the Suffering Servant who was so heartbreakingly mistreated. Jesus was not just a victim; He was the chief protago-
nist crafting every gesture, every word, making the drama say
exactly what He had intended from ages past. Jesus made a
stand. The cross plunged into the earth is above all an act of

Christ's will, a forceful declaration, an irrevocable choice to save us no matter what the cost.

## Making a Statement at the Cross

Christ's act was so decisive it reverberates through all history, affecting all mankind. "And by that will (Christ's), we have been made holy through the sacrifice of the body of Jesus Christ once for all" (Hebrews 10:10). This act of volition is our starting point in coming up with a will of our own. Of course Calvary is primarily about atonement; it's where we go to receive pardon and right standing with God. Nothing should diminish that. But it can also be a weapon. Scripture frequently and explicitly invites us to come to that cross and identify with the One who is making His statement there. In fact, we are asked to, somehow, die with Christ.

Jesus willed Himself to die; we're invited to share in that experience—with a hitch. Christ died *because* of sin; we're to die *to* sin. We're asked to stake a claim at the Place of the Skull, to make a stand: *I'm crucified with Christ, dead to sin, alive to God.*

In order to arouse our will, we first look at the cross. Don't look at the sin that's threatening you in order to beef up your will; don't look at your past record and moan; look at the cross. If you look carefully and prayerfully, you'll be inspired. After admiring Christ's gracious and courageous act of will, you can express solidarity with Him: *Yes, we're in this together; thank You that I can stand with You. By the power of the cross I claim that I am crucified to this sin, dead to it, and responsive to God.* Elie Wiesel once wrote, "Words can sometimes, in moments of grace, attain the quality of deeds." A good look at the cross gives us such a moment of grace; our statement becomes a deed.

Success in dealing with a habit starts when our will is inspired. If we try to start the fight on our own, simply on raw determination, we usually don't go very far; we're trying to jump-start a cold will. Instead, heat it up first at the cross. Identify with Christ: *Yes, I stand with you at Calvary. You died decisively, now help me do the same.* In this way you put the cross between yourself and the sin that's harassing you. As Paul explained, through the cross "the world has been crucified to me, and I to the world."

Think of will as a wedge which the cross drives between your old habit and its roots in you, its circuitry in your mind. The cross is what gives that wedge its momentum and leverage; the more clearly you identify with Christ crucified, the hotter that wedge becomes and the more effectively it separates you from a chronic sin.

## Statement Aimed at God

Don't try to go one-on-one with a habit. Always approach it through the crucified Christ. Practically speaking, this means that Jesus' act of will must loom larger in your thoughts than the ominous sin. That will happen if you start your efforts with a good look at the cross and with a good statement made toward Christ.

This is the best way I've found to understand the 100 percent/100 percent paradox and how we "place our will in God's hands." First of all, we're totally involved in making the statement; we say it altogether. But also, we say it to God altogether, not just at sin or at ourselves. Much of the difference between "works of the flesh" and "striving with God's strength" is simply who we're talking to. We can either harangue ourselves over a cold will or identify with the crucified God and find an inspired will. The person who hasn't placed his will in God's hands is talking to himself all the time or focusing on sin all the time. The person who has placed his will in God's hands is claiming a companion every step of the way. And when our will is exercised toward God, the door is thus opened for Him to act more decisively in us.

## Overcoming Inertia

There have been many varied attempts by Christians to carry out this injunction to be crucified with Christ, to mortify the flesh. A hermit named Dominic once jumped into a bush full of thorns and rolled around until he was bloody in order to clear his mind of lustful thoughts. It worked. But that's not a long-term solution. We can't keep abusing ourselves into purity.

The cross changes us by rewriting our minds. First, it gets us over the initial hurdle that knocks us down over and over again in our race to escape a habit: our aversion to unpleasantness. Sin is pleasant for a time — often it brings instant gratification, and our problem begins with inertia: going with the flow of our easiest impulses. Centuries ago Catherine of Siena said it well: "The soul, left to herself, makes a beeline for self-indulgence and is all ears for the song that betrays her."

In order to deal with a well-established habit, we have to buck inertia — that tendency to keep going in the same direction, or to remain embedded in a rut. We usually must put up with the discomfort of denying ourselves some supposed goody. Dominic did have a point; we need to be trained to accept a little pain.

This may not appear to be a very big hurdle, but masses of people do remain hopelessly herded into habits and securely corralled there by this flimsy knee-high fencing: what they feel like doing at the moment. That's it. The sturdy iron cage of something like heroin addiction is the exception. For most of us, our path through life is prescribed by mere nudgings of the flesh, the quickest urges; incredibly low barriers determine our destiny. And our contemporary push-button pleasures and wall-to-wall comforts don't train us for anything but easy street.

That's why the cross must arrive on the scene to divert that flow, to help us face unpleasantness. The sufferings of Christ overshadow our reluctance. If we try to face down a habit on our own, our natural tendency to avoid unpleasantness will loom large. That old rut invites us down irresistibly and we give in to the inertia of the sinful nature. But if we lead with the cross in confronting an old habit, then we approach discomfort from a very different perspective. John of the Cross advised, "Whenever anything disagreeable or displeasing happens to you, remember Christ crucified and be silent."

A good, steady look at Christ crucified makes sin appear much more avoidable. His heroic act of the will encourages us to make a statement: *Yes, I'm willing to hurt; I'm willing to let go of the sin that feels good at the moment.* That is our first step over the fencing that has corralled us for so long.

How do we crucify the flesh and mortify the sinful nature? Not by groaning about carnality, but by simply turning from it to something else. The great will that we need is always over there at Golgotha. Our strength comes from admiring Christ, claiming His death, calling on His decisive act, expressing solidarity with the One stretched out on the cross.

Paul shows the liberating significance of what seems, at first, a forbidding fact: "We had the sentence of death within ourselves in order that we should not trust in ourselves, but in God who raises the dead" (2 Corinthians 1:9). The sentence of death is a closed door; we no longer look back at our record of failure, but gaze steadily at the God who gives resurrected life.

Let's look at some specific guidelines for exercising an inspired will as opposed to a cold one.

### Put will at the beginning.

Unfortunately, most of us think about willpower only when in the thick of temptation. Staring at some prurient magazine cover, ready to feast on the flesh, we suddenly remember our will-to-purity and call it into action. But of course it's already vastly outnumbered by other impulses. Or having worked our nerves into a frayed knot after a bad day at the office, we find ourselves screaming at our spouse again and only then think about our will-to-patience, which is all but prostrate in the heat of our passion.

We do need to exercise our wills in the heat of spiritual battle. But it's infinitely better to pray for it early than yell for it late. Our will is best put to use at the beginning, as we start the day devotionally. That's when we need to reinforce our statement at the scene of the cross: *I am crucified with Christ*. Only then can we make our statement toward God instead of merely at sin. That gives us much more leverage to move temptation when it comes our way.

### Promise in steps.

Exercising our will often seems to involve promises. After a really bad moral fall we're apt to tell God, "I'll never do this again. Never again." In the aftermath, the sin seems so repulsive and our unfaithfulness to our Lord so painful that we feel compelled to make big vows. But then time passes, our zeal descends to a more sustainable level, and the old temptations drop by for a chat. We feel completely different now. The pull is just as strong as ever and, after fighting a bit on the way down, we succumb. Promise broken. Our betrayal feels even worse now.

Making earnest promises is a normal and healthy response to God in repentance, but they usually come back to accuse us and, as ropes of sand, mock all our future resolutions. I suggest making more short-term promises at first. Don't swear that you'll never do it again. Make promises in shorter, more doable steps. Make your earnest statement at the cross: *I am crucified with Christ; I consider myself dead to that sin and responsive to this godly quality.* Then promise God you will be back tomorrow at this time to make the same commitment. And the next day promise to return again. In the fervor of your repentance, concentrate that energy on immediate steps: *This is what I'll do today and tomorrow.*

By all means, tell the Lord that you desire more than anything else to never again fall into that miserable pit. Lay your heart out. But promise the specific, the immediate. Don't make heroic pledges at first that the enemy can use to dump on you later.

After you do establish a few successes, however, bigger promises can be useful. Staying "clean" for a month or a year, for example. But they are generally best phrased as goals rather than pledges: *Help me, Lord, to stay on this track every day of this month.*

I once asked the Lord for a year's furlough from my old porn nemesis, something which still bowled me over on rare occasions. He'd given me successful stands; the habit didn't threaten as it once did, but still it remained a potentially disastrous one hanging about the dark corners of my mind, and I wanted to establish one year of freedom. I set this out before the Lord as a goal, taking a stand with Him at the cross on a regular basis. And it proved to be a great year, not perfect, but very close. My stumbling did disappoint me, but at the end I wasn't so much devastated because I'd broken a promise as encouraged because a bigger goal had created a bigger momentum.

### Choose unconditionally.

One of the advantages of writing in our minds a clear, decisive statement at the scene of the cross is that we can better avoid the perils of conditional change. Often we subconsciously set up conditions that God must meet in order for us to obey Him.

I remember one very uncomfortable night when I was fighting jet lag in a city far from home and trying to go to sleep. Temptation knocked on the door and beckoned me outside and down to the hotel lobby where several girlie magazines waited impatiently. I fought it for some time, but I just couldn't go to sleep. After tossing and turning for hours, I began pleading that God would put me to sleep (out of my misery), and then almost demanded that He do so. In the end I slipped into an if/then state of the will without quite realizing it. If God would do His part and help me lose consciousness, then I would turn altogether from this temptation.

It wasn't until later that I saw I'd created an obstacle for God to jump over in order for me to be faithful. There are many subtle ways in which we try to force God to perform for us as a condition of obedience. Earnest pleas under duress, like,

"Speak to me now, Lord; please reveal Yourself," can actually be a subconscious demand that if the Lord doesn't zap us in some way, obliterating the temptation, we will have no choice but to give in.

To avoid this, we need to decide to obey God beforehand, no matter what unpleasantness we may face in the process. That is best done, again, as we're moved by the cross. Jesus' act of willful mercy despite all the abuse and ridicule that human beings and demons could heap on Him—that's our starting point. Who could possibly set up self-serving conditions after standing with the innocent One who gave His life away unconditionally for everyone else's sin? Expressing solidarity with Jesus on the cross, we prayerfully rewrite: *I am crucified with Christ; I am dead to this sin. No matter what obstacles it may throw in my way, I won't erect any in Your way.*

### Choose out loud.

As we keep taking our steps out of a habit, each day making our statement of intent at the cross, there is a danger that our will may become inaudible. That is, the repetition of those words about being crucified with Christ can slide into a semi-automatic ritual which doesn't register very well in our brains.

It's natural for us to start ignoring the familiar—the drone of a fan, the hum of traffic outside. Remember that circuitry in our minds which can tone down or tune out certain kinds of repeated stimuli? Our same old statements in prayer tend to slide imperceptibly from decisive words to memorized lines, and somewhere along the way our will actually bows out; we're no longer fully involved. It's possible after a while to mouth "Lord deliver me from this sin" and savor its charms at the same time.

So we have to consciously work to keep our stand at the cross fresh, something which makes a mark in our minds. Try to come to your prayer with a spirit of appreciation for the new things you see in the inexhaustible theme of Calvary. Then speak to God consciously, deliberately. God asks us to "draw near with a true heart," a heart carefully aimed at Him. Once in a while you may run into a text of fierce commitment that will help you speak more decisively—Job's resolution, for example: "If my step has turned from the way, or my heart followed my eyes, or if any spot has stuck to my hands, let me sow and another reap, and let my crops be uprooted."

Praying in an audible voice can also help us be more alert; adopting a different posture may help. Whatever we do, our expression of solidarity must always be out loud in a spiritual sense; even if it echoes only in our hearts, it must echo.

### Use failure.

Finally, never underestimate the value of desperation; your darkest hour of failure can lay the groundwork for a great comeback. One of the turning points in my life came one sultry summer day when I was confronted by my utter helplessness before the "big habit" that loomed over me. I could look back on a very long string of earnest struggles and shameful failures. That day brought the last straw; I had indulged in the pleasures of mass-produced flesh without even wanting to very badly. It had progressed to the point of compulsion and I was terrified by its casual way of toying with me.

In my fear and anguish, I dropped to my knees and spent hours pouring out my desperate straits before the Lord. I kept calling up to Him out of this dark pit I'd sunk into. Everything down there was just as the psalmist described it and I wanted out in the worst way.

Paradoxically, it was when I glimpsed the utter defeat of my will that I found a way to exercise it effectively; I finally got a place to stand. In that fervent and prolonged time of prayer, I invested a lot of mental and emotional energy in the One crucified for me. I took the Place of the Skull very seriously.

And that intense prayer did make a great difference. In the months, and even years, that followed, I found that some kind of will was inside me that hadn't been there before. God had placed significant distance between myself and this sin that considered me a pushover. It was as if the cross had been planted firmly and unconditionally in harm's way.

The despair I experienced that day is not something you want to sink into very often. It's a mistake to try to make yourself miserable on a regular basis. But at strategic moments, especially when we reach bottom and are ready to make a definite stand, desperation can be an invaluable aid to repentance.

Thank God for carving out a place for us to start at the cross. Let's not forget that the will is a very significant gift. It's not some vestigial organ within the fallen which we have no way of using meaningfully. God has created a place in history where we can exercise our will to great effect, where our feeble gesture is joined to His heroic act.

# 3

# A Self with Which to Fight

In 1980, just as Peru was struggling to make its way out of twelve years of dictatorship and toward full democracy, an engineering consultant named Hernando de Soto began to study two communities that stood on opposite banks of Lima's Rimac river. He was interested in them because they were located quite close together and yet presented marked contrasts. In the neighborhood called Carrión, the majority of the dwellings were crude huts made of mud bricks, or cardboard and plywood. Yet the residents were not exactly destitute; de Soto noticed refrigerators and other modern appliances visible through most open doorways and television antennas sprouting from almost all the shacks.

Across the river, in the sister community of Castilla, attractive three- and four-story brick homes bordered by tidy gardens and paved sidewalks dominated the scene. Many of the residents were merchants who lived above thriving businesses—a pharmacy, a grocery, a tire store, a shoe shop.

De Soto wanted to help rebuild his country and he'd been pondering the big economic questions: Why do some people prosper and others languish? Why are some nations poor, and others rich? So he began talking to residents, the police, and government officials. To his surprise he discovered that both these communities had almost identical beginnings. They'd been founded at the same time by Indian migrants who'd come from the same area, even the same villages. In fact, brothers were living across the river from each other.

So how to explain their vast economic differences? The usual answers wouldn't do. Both communities had the same cultural background. Both had been settled by migrants claiming squatter's rights over public lands. If foreign or local exploitation was involved, both seemed equally vulnerable to it.

Finally, de Soto tracked down a retired Housing Ministry official who'd seen the two neighborhoods develop for decades. He told de Soto about the crucial difference. The elected leader of the Castilla neighborhood had lobbied and pled with Lima's politicians for six long years until they granted land titles to the residents. Once secure from eviction, home owners borrowed, sweated, and saved until they could improve their dwellings. In ten years their homes had increased in value a phenomenal forty-one times that of untitled houses.

Residents across the river in Carrión remained only squatters on the land. They could not add and rent rooms or sell property or borrow money to set up businesses. So, logically enough, they spent their money on appliances and on pickup trucks to move everything if they were evicted.

De Soto realized that, in this case, the difference between poverty and prosperity was simply a matter of owning the ground under your feet. A dwelling had to belong to you in order for you to work at improving it.

This economic discovery tells us something very important about personal growth. We need to own the ground under our feet; we have to stake a claim to our dwelling if we are to improve it. In other words, if we are to change, we must be secure.

People without a strong sense of identity are too vulnerable to grow; they are too busy using appliances to prop up the cardboard shack that is their dwelling. The possibility of eviction always looms over them; they secretly fear their meager hold on a solid sense of self may slip away altogether.

Having a secure sense of identity is the spiritual equivalent to possessing a title to our homes. It's often the difference between poverty and prosperity in the personal realm. Whatever other factors may enter the picture — your background or exploitation by others — what you do about identity right now makes the crucial difference.

## I Am Not My Habit

Having a strong sense of identity is especially important when struggling with chronic sin because we often allow our unhealthy habits to define us. This is the opposite error of regarding a behavior pattern as some foreign object that happened to drop into the system. But in its effect, it's not that different. Both misperceptions end up giving aid and comfort to our adversary.

Generally, we don't allow the full-blown sin itself to define us; very few people want to be nailed to the wall as an adulterer or a liar. But we do cozy up to their less obvious lethal allies: "I'm just weak-willed; I can't help myself." "I've got a temper; that's just me." We begin to see a particular weakness as part of our personality, perhaps even part of what makes us endearing to our friends.

When we start looking at ourselves through our habits, we lose the ability to confront them — at arms length. A bit of distance is important in beginning to deal with a habit. If we feel that, by attacking certain chronic behaviors we're actually hacking away at our human essence, then our efforts will most likely be sabotaged at some point, consciously or unconsciously. We fear becoming an amputated version of ourselves.

It's very important to own a habit, *but it's equally important not to allow ourselves to be identified by it*. Confession solves the first problem: We acknowledge that the habit is in us, maybe deep in us. But now we must see that we are much more than this sin. It doesn't sum us up, or even label us meaningfully.

## The Redeemer's Point of View

Here's where God's perspective takes on enormous significance. Our Savior defines us according to our potential. He doesn't see us locked into a pattern we've developed; He emphasizes our possibilities. Listen to how He labels saints with sinful tendencies. We're identified as children of God, called to be holy in the same way that He is, assured that our citizenship is in heaven. We're God's chosen; He has anointed us, set His seal of ownership on us, and placed His own Spirit within us as a foretaste of future glories. We're vessels to be used for noble purposes, temples of God. The Father boasts about doing more than we can imagine through the power at work inside us. Most incredible of all, we're described as God's rich and glorious inheritance.

This is the essential New Testament anthem which celebrates our identity. Through image after image, God tries to make His perspective sink in so that we don't just see ourselves through our mistakes, however habitual, but see ourselves as what we can *become*.

Let's face it, at times this can be tough to do while burdened with some chronic transgression. Looking back over a pattern of sin which fades into the far horizon, and down at your feet still aligned with it, you do tend to unwittingly slouch into the rut and just "be yourself." We've got to really get an earful from this Lord who shouts about His leverage, about our possibilities in Him. That's got to be a big idea in our minds, something which the Spirit writes in our "innermost place." In relationship with God, our potential *is* as vast as His character. All these New Testament metaphors are true, not just some therapeutic pretense. We *can* become holy by maintaining close contact with Him. His sky is the limit.

And so, before we go out to pick our fight with that all-too-familiar bullying sin, we've got to see ourselves as the Redeemer does—and keep on seeing ourselves that way when the action heats up. *I am not just weak-willed. I may have wimped out under certain pressures in the past, but that doesn't mean that's me, period. I may have a tendency toward adulterous fantasies, but that doesn't define me.*

Don't put in concrete what you are; that only makes you defensive. Stare instead at what you are becoming in Christ. People are not one thing, or one pattern of things. We are not irrevocably fixed by those synaptic junctions in our brains which have decreed smooth flow or resistance. Other junctions are constantly being created. We are fluid; we don't have to keep adding to the same old lines in the brain.

Instead, etch in those new lines about adoption as sons and daughters, salt of the earth, light of the world, apples of His eye, jewels sparkling in His hand. Fix God's descriptions firmly in your mind. Create and memorize a psalm of identity. Make it your own; keep adding to it; keep discovering new glimpses of who you are in Christ.

## A Self with Which to Fight

In traditional Christian teaching about "growing in Christ," self has served more or less as the enemy. We typically hear injunctions about combating self-will, overcoming self, and stamping out our desires wherever they may flare up. Self is portrayed as the big obstacle that needs to be removed in order for us to get to God's will and His graces.

There is much truth in this, of course. It's possible to use self as a synonym for sinful nature. And selfishness *is* one of our most basic problems, no question about it. But sometimes the shots we take at our self can backfire.

General "Stonewall" Jackson trained his men of the First Brigade to respond in battle immediately and cohesively as a fighting unit; they became one of the Confederacy's most devastating war machines. In May of 1863, Jackson succeeded in outmaneuvering Union general Joseph Hooker and won a decisive victory near Chancellorsville, Virginia. But then, as he was riding back through dense woods from the attack, Jackson was shot three times—by his own men. The general had given strict orders before the battle to shoot any unknown soldiers, and ask questions later. His well-disciplined men had done just that.

Many struggling believers seem to follow very similar orders in relating to any desire or impulse or stray thought that arises from the self. Shoot first, ask questions later. Unfortunately, the general, our volitional leader, is sometimes the one felled. It's possible to beat down the self in such a way that little is left to respond to the call to stand up and fight against evil. If we drill the self into going limp every time a desire wells up within it, how is it supposed to be resilient and tough in battle? If we try to turn the self into a benign zero, no one is going to be home when God knocks on the door to dwell within us.

So it's important to make a distinction between our identity as a self, and our sinful nature. This is not to say that our sinfulness can be compartmentalized and kept away from some pure essence in our souls. Sin has thoroughly tainted us; we're imperfect, period. But God does want to get a handle on me, myself. I must be able to say "Here I am" when He calls. We retain the image of God within us, however flawed and distorted it may have become. We do make significant choices.

So, in practical terms, how do we become a secure self and still get serious about opposing our sinful nature? First by surrender. When the human self confronts the Living God, unconditional surrender is required. Nothing can be held back from Him. We're the patient on the table, opened up by the laser light of God's omniscience. We don't presume to tell the One who created our unique personality where and when He may cut and heal the psyche.

But there is a difference between unconditional surrender and zero. We say, "Here I am, Lord, here's all of me; re-create me more fully into Your image." We don't say, "I'm nobody; I'm worthless." That prepares the ground for defeat. Alone, cut off from God, we spiral down into spiritual oblivion. But in close communion with Him, identified as His child, we can participate in the divine nature.

God wants a secure self He can work with, and He helps create that by defining us in terms of our possibilities. We decide to eradicate an unhealthy habit not because it's one more evidence of our wretched character but because it doesn't fit into a very clear sense of who we are.

The apostle Paul is an excellent example here. He did not hesitate to admit his very painful mistakes in the past and his struggles with "the law of sin and death" in the present, but he also had a strong sense of identity and mission. Forgetting all the patterns of sin that lay behind him, he pressed on toward the goal of an upward call. His confident affirmation can be ours: "I am what I am by God's grace."

## *At God's Right Hand*

### Filling In the Holes

Another reason a clear sense of identity is so helpful in dealing with chronic sin is that habits are often attempts to compensate for some sense of inadequacy, attempts to fill in a hole somewhere in our self-concept.

The typical example is the overweight person who stuffs his face whenever he feels depressed. If friends seem a bit distant, a crunchy chocolate bar can always stand in for love. But there are many other examples. Adulterous fantasies sometimes cover over uncertainties about manhood. Indulging in flashes of rage can also give macho currency to men who fear they may be running a bit short. A pattern of self-pity which sinks into depression may be a person's attempt to get attention from a spouse. People typically use biting criticism as a weapon against being put down themselves, and wield gossip as a way to identify those on the outside who keep them on the inside.

We're all trying to take care of business, trying to fill the holes. Many of us have aching needs conceived in a family background woefully short on nurture and healthy affection. Insecurity in general is fertile breeding ground for all kinds of habits and compulsions.

Overcoming those habits on a long-term basis requires us to fill the holes in the right way. We need to invest time and energy in contemplating God's love. And God has created an ideal place in which we may do that; it appears in the book of Ephesians. In chapter two Paul tells believers what happens to us the moment we place our faith in Jesus as Savior. The apostle reveals that God makes us "alive with Christ" even while we are "dead in transgressions." While we are still full of the old sinful patterns, still locked in the stupefying embrace of the flesh, God resurrects us with Christ. He begins pouring His spiritual life into us and, even more importantly, counts us every bit as spiritually alive and whole as His perfect Son arising from the grave.

We share in Christ's resurrection in the sense of being completely identified with it in God's eyes. And what's more, we also share in His ascension. Paul says, "And God raised us up with Christ and seated us with Him in the heavenly realms in Christ Jesus."

This is past tense, according to Paul, something that already happened — at the moment when the Christian life began, when believers were still doomed in their habitual transgressions. That's when the miracle of justification occurs — God accepts us in His beloved Son, righteous and complete. And when God accepts, He does so completely. We are *in* Christ, period. If Christ was resurrected, we're resurrected. If Christ ascended, then we've ascended, in God's eyes. If Christ is seated in triumph at God's right hand after His heroic exploits on earth, then we are sitting right there with Him, counted as God's Right-Hand Woman, God's Right-Hand Man.

Why? Because of His "great love for us." Because He is "rich in mercy." God Almighty gives us the most coveted position in the entire universe — the honored place beside His throne. A sea with the crystal gleam of ice spreads at our feet. An emerald rainbow shimmers above us. God Almighty, whose face is as the sun in its strength, whose arms and feet are like burnished bronze, sits beside us. Sanctuary beings ceaselessly declare how holy, holy, holy is the One who was, is, and is to come. This is our privileged place right now, even with those chronic sins loitering about, even with the embarrassing habit lurking near, we are cherished in the Beloved.

We are not welcomed up into heaven and into the awesome throne room because we've finally overcome all our sins; the welcome is not a recognition of some achievement. We haven't "arrived" in an experiential sense. We've "arrived" in the sight of God — and that's what matters most.

## The Dying Swan

Anna Pavlova, a Russian ballet superstar of the early 1900s, awed audiences around the world with her incomparable technique and grace. She has been acclaimed as the greatest ballerina of all time. Anna's farewell performance at the Apollo Theatre in London was perhaps her most memorable. She was to play the role she made famous, the Dying Swan. But tragically, the great ballerina succumbed to pneumonia and died two days before the event.

Still, on the appointed night, the Apollo Theatre was packed. The orchestra began playing, the curtain rose, a spotlight flashed through the dark, and the entire audience rose to its feet. They all stood gazing into the pool of light as it wandered around the stage, accompanied by the orchestral theme. They all remembered the luminous dance of this "ethereal maiden" in white with the flashing dark eyes. And when the music stopped at last, they gave the vanished Anna a thunderous ovation that echoed on and on in the night.

In his own unique role as something of a Dying Swan, Jesus Christ gave the universe an unforgettable performance. I see thunderous applause coming from the Father and the heavenly beings, giving tribute to the beloved Son. But then this performer vanishes and only a pool of light remains — on the stage of God's throne room. The miracle is that we are invited to stand in that pool of light — and the Father keeps on applauding. He sees His beloved Son performing still. The incomparable grace of the Son lives on and, as it were, covers us.

Our place at God's right hand can become another visual cue that triggers a series of healthy responses and turns suggestions of poor self-worth into background noise. This is where we start filling in those aching holes that keep sucking us down.

So do some rewriting. Affirm your position in Christ: *I am cherished, complete in the beloved Son, seated at God's right hand. That's the place where I am most truly "me."* Don't settle for anything less. Meditate on this, your essential position in life. Here's where we can absorb that deep and wide love, the love that never gives up, which woos the adulterous wife, weeps over recalcitrant Jerusalem, extends its arms on the cross in spite of all the mockery, and spreads over us as vast as the heavens.

## Catching Providences

Another way we apprehend this divine regard is by keeping an eye out for God's providences in our daily life. Quite a few believers complain that they never really see Him act on their behalf. They hear about His great miracles elsewhere, but He never seems to show His hand to them. Part of the reason for this is simply our passivity. We sit around waiting for God to do some trick for us. But He most often appears in the thick of things, popping up wherever people are trying to reach others, dropping in where people are earnestly struggling with temptation.

And if we rarely see God in action, it's often our own eyes that are at fault. We miss a lot of little things. We pass off His subtle nudges, His quiet gestures of love.

Fred was a sixties junkie in prison trying to stabilize himself after many losing bouts with hard drugs. A few months before his imprisonment, he had accepted Christ as his Savior, but still found it hard to refuse a shot of heroin — it had been tough going on the outside. Now in jail he was trying to get his act together with Jesus. The Gospel of John was really starting to sink in; Fred felt blessed by it.

But then he heard that his buddy Manny had persuaded his wife to smuggle in some heroin on one of her visits. The guys were planning to get loaded.

All the old impulses fired up again and Fred felt gutted by his old habit. He prayed in weak desperation, telling God just how vulnerable he felt, not really thinking he could withstand the temptation. Then he had lunch and went to a chapel service. Back in his cell he climbed on his bunk, began reading the Gospel of John again, and fell asleep.

Hours later Fred awakened to the sounds of his buddies talking about what good stuff that was. "What do you mean? What happened?" he asked.

A glazed-eyed Manny looked at him, surprised. "Oh wow, aren't you loaded? I thought you were coasting, man."

As it turned out, everyone had gotten so excited about shooting up they'd forgotten about Fred. Suddenly this junkie woke up to what seemed "heavy evidence." God had enabled him to survive the irresistible. Fred seized this evidence with all his strength: "We were partners. I found out something was really going on with God. It was tangible. I didn't always lie down and read the Gospel of John and go to sleep, but that day I did. If I'd been awake I'd have geezed; it's just a kind of reflex."

But then a feeling-no-pain buddy interrupted his reverie: "There's still a real good wet cotton."

It was lying there on the table, a bit of leftover heroin, not enough to get really high on, but something of a rush nonetheless. Fred, however, had seen a bit of God's care for him, up close and personal. He wasn't just a junkie anymore: "Suddenly I realized that God had more to offer than a wet cotton."

Fred told his buddy, "No, man, I don't want it." They all stared at him without comprehending. He continued, "I'll never shoot again."

Lifted up in a new sense of self, Fred found himself vow-ing with fervor: "I'd rather die than stick a needle in my arm." This decision proved potent; it "fortified all the previous mickey mouse decisions I had made. Right there I hung on to God and God hung on to me."

Not everyone would have seen an afternoon nap as a providential gift. Some might have missed God's love-in-action completely and seen only the problem. But Fred used God's nudge to become more than his habit. As he recalled: "At times I had tried to get out of the doper bag. I'd done whatever I could: use my head, enter a sanitarium, read good books, join the service, get new friends, go to school, take TV training. I thought these things would make me an out. But when I'd get someplace else, doing other things, I'd still have the same head, the same inclinations, the same drives, the same hang-ups, the same everything."

Finally, however, through one small revelation, Fred felt himself in partnership with God. They were together. And this new identity would see him through — all the way to freedom, a new family, and the gospel ministry.

Keep an eye out for God's care. Be thankful for the small blessings that flow your way every day. It's this kind of recep-tivity that will make God's love pop right out at you where before you only saw the same old one-dimensional routine.

Remember, we're God's children, not only because of a holy calling to be like Him, but also because we are His creation, period. Nothing we ever do can diminish the passionate de-sire He has for us as a divine parent. God does not love us because He has worked so hard to see our spiritual potential; He sees spiritual potential because He loves us so greatly.

## Summary: The Core Circles

As a review of what we've covered so far, let's look at one example of the rewriting process. Take those of us who frequently lose our temper and who have trouble seeing our-selves apart from the habit. We start with a stimulus — say an encounter with an obnoxious co-worker. That event could fire off any one of countless thought, emotion, and action pathways laid out in our brains. We've represented that infinitely complex network involving millions of neurons with a vastly simplified diagram.

The initial stimulus will invariably follow whatever pathway fires first and strongest. All of us react to events through some response pattern that has worn a groove over time in which certain impulses flow freely, almost automatically.

If a faulty identity script is recorded in our minds, we will tend to respond to the pressure to express destructive anger with the self-reinforcing pattern pictured here in figure 1. It's a bit like completing an electric circuit; whichever thought pattern dominates the center of our attention wins. We represent this as a circle, even though of course there are no nice neat circles within our brains.

In our example, we do have an alternative pathway in place, but it's lightly etched in as mere resistance: "Hold back." That groove is not deep enough to divert the flow of other belligerent thoughts. So the completed thought-circuit goes on demanding "Blow up," loud and clear.

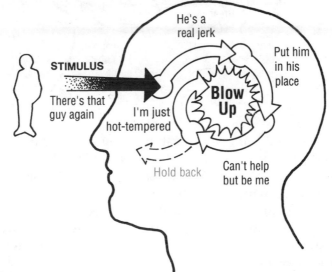

FIGURE 1

But what if we have done some rewriting about our identity through our prayerful interaction with the Word? As we appreciatively absorb the names which God gives us—from the heady perspective of God's throne room—a deeper groove is formed in our minds than the previous one about our chronic failure. Remember, we can't completely erase established pathways, but we can form detours around them. Now when the same stimulus comes, we don't have to react in panic or fury; we simply turn to the alternate channel (see figure 2). Our response revolves around how Christ relates to us and to other people. The self-reinforcing, completed circuit fires off a very different dominant message: "Extend Christ's grace."

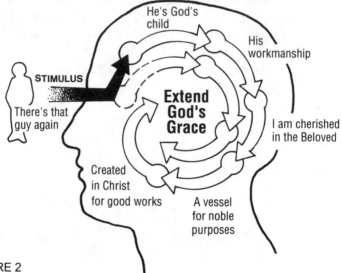

FIGURE 2

The great thing about establishing such a pattern in our minds is that it can continually expand. That happens as we actively respond to healthy messages and build on them. It's not simply a matter of chanting certain key phrases over and over. Remember that identically repeated stimuli tend to be ignored after a while. The neuroreceptors react: "Okay, okay, pipe down." Deliberate, creative response is what reinforces the message and deepens the channels. In this case, we thank God for His manifold love; we enjoy His gracious regard and catch new signs of His providential care. As we build on our identity in Christ, this circle of thought takes over more and more pathways, firing off more and more responses. As a result, it grows farther out to the edges of conscious thought. We are able to pick up negative stimuli much earlier and can therefore counter a habitual reaction much more quickly.

Each one of the strategies covered in the first three chapters involves this kind of expansive rewriting. Each one results in a self-reinforcing response pattern that we will picture simply as a circle. So far we've looked at three essential themes—agreeing with God, making a stand at the cross, and seeing ourselves through God's eyes—which form internal scripts related to our innermost thoughts and attitudes. These core circles overturn a habit by firing off healthy, alternative responses related to confession, will, and identity.

Chapter 1 dealt with the components of a healthy confession script.

### Honest agreement, not persuasion
> Agree with the God who knows you intimately and loves you infinitely.
> Confess in a sanctuary setting.
> Acknowledge that sin is costly and that pardon is complete.

### Renewing repentance
> Seek the sorrow that leads to life.
> Value (don't imitate) the atonement as a finished work.

This circle of confession expands to push that labyrinth of self-serving excuses and free-floating guilt farther and farther out from our innermost, purposeful thoughts. It creates more and more room for an affirmation of mercy and redemption (see figure 3).

Chapter 2 presented a script on exercising our will.

### Use what you have
> Your total involvement.
> God's total involvement.

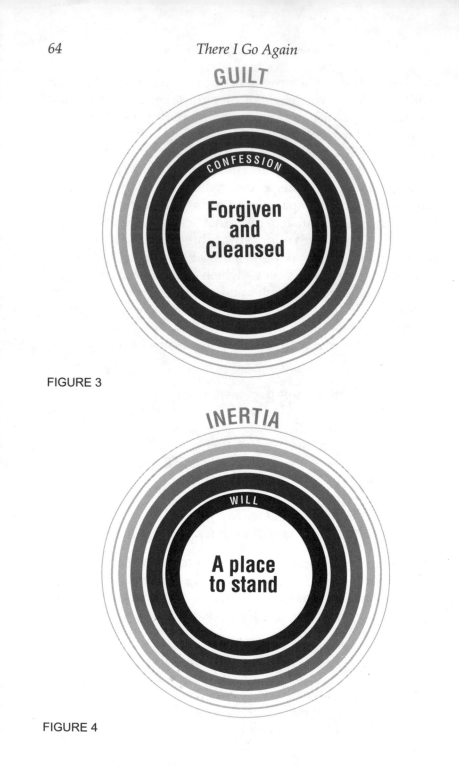

GUILT

CONFESSION

**Forgiven
and
Cleansed**

FIGURE 3

INERTIA

WILL

**A place
to stand**

FIGURE 4

**How to stand**
> Make a statement of solidarity with Christ.
> Make it toward God (not just at yourself).
> Make it at the cross, with Christ's heroic act of will.

**Exercising an inspired will**
> Put will at the beginning.
> Promise in steps.
> Choose unconditionally and out loud.

As we build up this circle of will, it takes over neural pathways, expanding in our minds to push the inertia of the carnal nature farther and farther out to the periphery and create more and more room for a strong stand with Christ at the cross (see figure 4).

Chapter 3 laid out a script related to our sense of self.

**God's point of view**
> You are much more than this habit.
> The Father cherishes you as His child.
> You have a self with which to fight.

**Renewing identity**
> See yourself at God's right hand, lifted up in Christ.
> Keep an eye out for God's providential care.

This circle of identity expands to push those holes in the self farther and farther from our innermost being (see figure 5). The wounds are healed. More and more room is created for an affirmation of our position in Christ.

These three core circles are not isolated patterns in our minds, of course. They become mutually reinforcing as they expand. The circle of confession, which leads our counterattack, is given impetus by the energetic conviction of a determined stand with the Crucified One. And the circle of will, in turn, is propelled outward by a confident awareness of our identity in Christ (see figure 6).

Any temptation or negative thought pattern must break through these expansive circles in order to capture our center

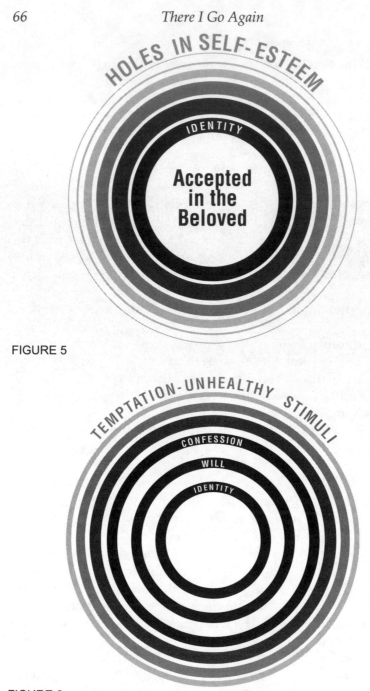

FIGURE 5

FIGURE 6

of attention and pull us back to the habit. The arrows of the enemy must somehow disrupt honest confession, then outflank our standing with Christ at the cross, and finally confront our secure sense of who we are.

## Wall of Fire

Traditionally we have pictured Christian warfare in terms of a shield, a rampart, a fortress within which we fend off the attacks of the enemy. I believe the new covenant of the law written in our hearts and minds changes our basic strategy. It enables us to work within a different kind of wall.

During the time when a lonely, harassed group of returned Hebrew exiles were attempting to rebuild a Jerusalem devastated by the Babylonians, they received an encouraging divine promise through Zechariah. In one of the prophet's visions, a man went out to measure Jerusalem and determine its precise length and width. An angel interrupted this work with these words: "Jerusalem will be a city without walls because of the great number of men and livestock in it. And I myself will be a wall of fire around it," declares the Lord, "and I will be its glory within" (Zechariah 2:4–5). The ragged remnant of Israel was told that Jerusalem would become a great, prosperous city; it would grow to such an extent that conventional walls could not enclose it. God Himself would act as a wall around her, not a static, defensive mass of stone, but an expanding bulwark of fire, lifted up as a direct extension of His glory within the city, centered in the holy sanctuary.

This glorious wall of fire is our model for spiritual warfare. We want to keep expanding and growing because of God's presence within us—not just manning the ramparts because of all the intimidating threats out there. We need circles of offense, not just defensive perimeters. God's dynamic Word can be written in as a healthy, positive flame of the Spirit in our minds.

# 4

# Counterpoint Virtues

A HABITUALLY tardy boy who slipped into his classroom late again explained that the icy streets were so slippery that whenever he tried to move a step forward he'd slide two steps back. The teacher thought this a sorry excuse. "If that were true," she asked, "how did you ever get to school?"

The boy replied brightly, "I finally turned around and went home!"

It's time to deal directly with our chronic habit and begin our strategy of replacing it. And we do that best not by struggling against our slippery adversary, but by turning around toward where we really want to go. If in trying to eliminate some habit from your life you find yourself slipping backwards, try facing the opposite direction: away from the sin and toward its antithesis.

We outmaneuver a habit primarily by adopting a counterpoint virtue as our visible goal. Think of the kid who's just learning to ride a bike and is trying his best to go in a straight line. Often he'll glare resolutely at the bushes he's determined to avoid — and end up wobbling right into them. Even though we may be trying to overcome a certain habit, we shouldn't primarily aim at it; we need to fix our gaze on exactly where we want to go — the more positive our goal the better.

## Think of a Man Not Shaving

Jesus once warned His very religious hearers of a rather peculiar danger. An evil spirit can be summarily dismissed from its habitual dwelling in a person, He said, but it will always come back after a while to check out its old comfortable haunt. And if it finds the dwelling unoccupied, albeit with floor swept clean and furniture neatly arranged, it will take this as an irresistible invitation, crash in, and throw a wild party with seven other spirits even roudier than itself. No one's home, why not?

Just getting up enough godly sorrow and earnest will to kick evil out is not enough. If our orientation is merely such things as not being unfaithful, not losing our temper, not gossiping, not sinking into self-pity, then we're just working on a vacancy. We may have swept the floor and cleared the coffee table, but cleanliness alone creates an unstable condition, a vacuum, and old habits are invariably the first to take advantage of it. Clearly, booting out the offending spirit in the first place *is* vitally important. We can't do without that step. But if we don't go on from there, we'll have taken one step forward in preparation for two steps back.

Mnemonists, people who specialize in memorizing things, typically "see" the list of numbers or names they are commiting to memory. They learn to associate them with concrete images, because visible objects are stored much more quickly and efficiently in our neural network than numbers or abstractions. Scientists who study the work of mnemonists to better understand how the brain works sometimes speculate on objects of thought which cannot be transformed into images — perfectly reasonable ideas which nevertheless don't register visually.

Take the statement, "I'm thinking of a man not shaving." Although it sounds odd, the sentence has a definite meaning. However, if you try to imagine a man not shaving, you come up blank. A negative concept just doesn't generate an image very easily, even though, of course, we use negative ideas (not doing certain things) all the time. "I am not going to work." What image does that bring to mind? Certainly not anything as specific as the phrase, "I'm going to work." You immediately visualize someone driving on the freeway or sitting in a bus reading a newspaper.

There's no doubt that forming vivid mental pictures makes remembering easier. That's important to consider in rewriting our minds. We can't write in negative concepts very well; they don't register as easily as positive ones. If you hear, "I'm thinking of a man not shaving," about all you can imagine is a man in a bathroom with a razor; the picture is still of shaving. Likewise with trying to focus on not losing my temper, not lusting, not falling into depression—it's the temper and the lust and the depression that register most in our minds, even though they're stated in the negative.

## The Power of Hidden Treasure

Too often our image of "being good" is merely an empty space on the other side of some clear and present sin. We don't really have a clear and present alternative. In Christ's parable of the hidden treasure, a tenant farmer plowing up a field ran over a pile of gold and silver someone had stashed away. Jesus said that the man "in his joy went and sold all he had and bought that field." This farmer liquidated all his worldly possessions in order to get something else, something worth a whole lot more. He didn't sell all in order to experience poverty. He was after a treasure. Similarly, the merchant who found a pearl of great value eagerly disposed of everything he had in order to purchase this one magnificent gem.

These parables apply principally to the initial act of the Christian life: choosing Jesus and His kingdom over and above everything else. But I think they also illuminate the subsequent acts of the Christian life: progressing in that kingdom. We get rid of our chronic sins, those encumbering possessions, in order to acquire something else infinitely more valuable.

We certainly could use a gold-mine mentality. The farmer and the merchant were compelled to pawn off their every trinket just as quickly as they could because their eyes were bulging out and their hearts fibrillating after this fortuitous find, this stroke of luck, this treasure lying there just waiting. Hating sin cannot produce the joy that compels us to sell all; only a treasure can.

The master of all these evil spirits works very hard to keep us from running into hidden treasure and apprehending its real value. Do a little sweeping—no big deal. Align the sofas—fine. But please don't look at that treasure. Our adversary knows that once we see that gold and silver glisten, his revolving door of spirits and habits gets jammed. Finding some pearl of a virtue is what motivates us best and longest, not just disposing of our carnal comforts. If all we see on the other side of our familiar nemesis is some nice clean vacuum, it'll be rough going getting him out the door—and he'll always be back knocking. The evil spirit should be kicked out because we've found a wonderful new roommate, one who makes the old freeloader look like death warmed over.

## Winning Hands Down

So we need to zero in on some counterpoint virtue that can serve as our motivating hidden treasure, a positive image that will stick in our minds. We need qualities that compel. The usual candidates don't always stand up under pressure too well. Traits like self-control and purity typically line up as opposites for any number of habits. But these virtues can appear quite colorless compared to juicy tidbits of gossip or the fiery insistence of a bad temper or the gaudy pull of lust. In fact, self-control and purity as we usually picture them aren't so much counterpoint virtues as anti-sins. Self-control is not bursting out with this or that. Purity is not indulging in this or that. They don't stand alone as ends in themselves; they don't have the pull of hidden treasure.

During my freshman year in college, I trudged up a long hill with a mixture of fear and expectation toward a small white house a few blocks from campus. It was a hot, quiet evening under a vast, moonless sky. Some students were having a prayer meeting there, purported to be of a most unusual nature.

Feeling rather vulnerable, I entered the house and was met by wall-to-wall students sitting on the floor, all singing heartily. I sat down and listened to their lively tunes; these kids meant every word. I sensed an amiable spirit in the room, as if you could know others there immediately and deeply.

Then a junior religion major stood up and began drawing diagrams on a whiteboard. He talked enthusiastically about how our sexual nature is related to the spirit, soul and body concept in Scripture. The Bible shows us just how healthy relationships progress, he said. First one establishes spiritual oneness with the other person. You grow together on that level. Then you progress through a mental and emotional give-and-take. And finally when that bonding process leads to a commitment, you become physically one. Genuine oneness in the flesh is a climax of the intimacy that has preceded it.

The guy spoke as if the principles of the Bible were the last word on sexuality. I was entranced by this beautiful and coherent picture of what God intended human oneness to be.

All my life, growing up in Christian schools, I'd heard about sexual morality in terms of venereal disease and unwanted pregnancy. You waited until marriage in order to avoid certain calamities. It had never occurred to me that purity could be anything but slightly embarassed defensiveness. There in that little white frame house, however, God's positive image of sexuality won hands down over everything else.

That night proved to be a turning point in my life; I definitely warmed up to "things of the Spirit" which before had seemed remote and forbidding. And there I experienced for the first time the power of virtue as hidden treasure to pursue.

## Ends in Themselves

Let's look at a few habits and try to come up with qualities possessing enough life and leverage to move out those offending spirits who've been proclaiming squatter's rights for so long.

### Solid Sensitivity

A problem that causes a great deal of struggle and anguish, and one that seems to stand out most in this age of the graphic image, is lust, the habit of relating to physically attractive people as sex objects. A good counterpoint virtue for misdirected passion is suggested to us by Paul's description of certain Ephesian apostates: "Having lost all sensitivity, they have given themselves over to sensuality. . . ." Here two qualities are presented as opposites: sensitivity and sensuality. The first looks deeper and deeper into a person, the second reduces the other to a kind of sign, a certain shape that stimulates. Lust is reductionistic, seeking ever more jolting stimuli for its ever decreasing response. But sensitivity aims at the whole; it attempts to picture a complete human being from the fragments of a person that usually catch our eye.

Sensitivity is the opposite of the condition Paul informed young Timothy about: "But the widow who lives for pleasure is dead even while she lives." Sensuality "wars against the soul"; it deadens our capacities to feel more than the lowest common denominator of the flesh. Those who feel the most are alive from the inside out and relate to others from the inside out.

We might call this quality *solid sensitivity*, since it has to have tenacity in order to push beyond the seductive distractions on the surface. There is a kind of sensitivity which connotes a fragile, sponge-like existence that absorbs everything passively. But here we mean a pearl of another color; the sensitivity that outmaneuvers lust has got to be tough, resilient. It's got to have weight, the ability to sink through the veneer and reach the heart.

Solid sensitivity is more than an opposite of sin; it helps solve the problem of lust. If, for example, I am able to pay steady attention to what's happening inside a girl, I will have bypassed my instinct to check her out as a piece of meat.

So when lust is the obstacle in your way, you can select solid sensitivity as your hidden treasure. That's where you want to go. Do some rewriting. To make solid sensitivity a clear and present picture, dig into Scripture and find verses that capture your imagination.

Now you can go out aiming to:

- Treat "younger women as sisters, with absolute purity."
- See every human being through the redemption of Jesus Christ.
- Feel one outstanding debt: to love one another (without hypocrisy).
- Continually "remember before our God" the good qualities I observe in others.
- Regard others with the knowledge that He has chosen me, and I possess a high calling.
- Focus on what will "encourage one another and build each other up."
- See God eye-to-eye, with a pure heart.
- Keep my mind sharp to seek out the true and noble, the just and gracious, the virtuous and excellent.

One image in particular seems to me to embody the essence of solid sensitivity. Speaking of spiritual sight, Jesus once told a crowd: "Your eye is the lamp of your body. When your eyes are good, your whole body also is full of light. But when they are bad, your body also is full of darkness" (Luke 11:34). I know how thoroughly an eye full of lust can suffocate spiritual life. But a sound and clear eye, the perspective of solid sensitivity, can continually illuminate all our relationships. I want to have that lamp burning bright.

## Jesus Alone

Some believers maintain that the secret of success is to forget about all these virtues and pursue Jesus alone. After all, isn't that what we're really after? The power is in Him, not in some moral category. They have a point. We do need to seek Jesus more than anything else. The problem is that it's easy for us, within our limited human perceptions and barren moral environment, to turn Jesus into an empty set. He can become the religious symbol lifted up whom we faithfully salute but don't really absorb as a living character. Any category left alone in our minds will slowly be drained of content. The living Christ can become just a word, an abstraction gradually bleached of living color.

Jesus is a very particular person. And qualities like solid sensitivity are what make up His specific character; it's one of the virtues that makes Him who He is. Zeroing in on a specific trait as our goal is not necessarily something different from aiming at Christ. True, we can come to regard the trait as just an isolated moral quality; that's why it's important to precede our aim with a stand on Golgotha. We first identify ourselves with the crucified Christ, with His death and life. But then we can focus on moral qualities from Scripture, especially from the New Testament, as highlights of Christ's person.

Sometimes a certain trait stands out in the gospel narrative itself. Jesus telling His disciples that these runny-nosed kids they are trying to nudge off to the side are really the centerpiece of His message, leading the rest of us into the kingdom as its first citizens — that shows me a wonderfully solid sensitivity that penetrates through a child's inconsequential exterior to a quality of spontaneous faith within. There are many other examples: Christ building up the woman who washed His feet while others, automatically fixed on the "ill-repute" label, were putting her down; Jesus transforming forever the epithet "Samaritan" into something good.

Uncovering and highlighting these moral qualities helps us revive the symbol in our minds. "We all, with unveiled face beholding as in a mirror the glory of the Lord, are being transformed into the same image from glory to glory. . . " (2 Corinthians 3:18, NASB). The glory of God is the glow of His sterling character. Making one of His qualities clear in our minds is a way to turn God from a remote abstraction to a transforming image.

## Malleability

How about another familiar nemesis: losing your temper, flashing out in anger and hurting people. What can stand in illuminating opposition to this problem?

If we look carefully at our outbursts of anger we'll notice that we generally blow our top because we're immovable in some way. An obstacle arises — we can't get this blankety-blank oil filter to budge, we can't get this kid to stop crying, we can't get through this line fast enough — and we keep banging ourselves against the impediment, becoming more heated with every exertion, until we explode. Outbursts of abusive anger typically arise from a one-track, straight-ahead fix on what we want. When this irresistible force meets some immovable object, a violent collision occurs.

What I've found most necessary in my struggle with un-healthy anger is a hold on the quality of *malleability*. I need to be malleable, moldable. George Eliot wrote: "It's easy finding reasons why other folks should be patient." The malleable find reasons for themselves. God advises us to relate to trials and obstacles as opportunities for growth, not just as opponents to wrestle to the ground. He often intends to teach us something valuable through the very irritant that we flail against. God must bend and shape us through what we bump against. If we remain rigid when confronted with an obstacle, we'll never grow; we just sink into a pattern where outbursts and inflex-ibility reinforce each other.

Being malleable is a counterpoint virtue which helps solve the problem of abusive anger. That's what we need to aim at — that specific part of Christ's character. After all, He used the most horrifying kind of obstacle, death by crucifixion, as a means of overcoming mankind's great tragedy. He was stretched out in agony by this trial, but He made it reshape Him into open-armed Savior.

As a matter of fact, Jesus spent three and a half years patiently re-molding one of His greatest obstacles: the minds of His disciples. Slow to understand, slower to believe, many times their growth in Christ's kingdom seemed to proceed at a glacial pace. But the Master worked on this bottleneck; He didn't yell at it or just try to pound some sense into it; He lived out His lessons over and over until finally, posthumously, they sank in at Pentecost.

Blessed are the malleable; they don't bang their heads against the wall; they find a new direction. If outbursts of anger are a chronic problem, fix this quality firmly in your mind through the positive images of Scripture:

- As God's chosen one, I clothe myself with gentleness and patience.
- Under duress, I claim the peace of Christ acting as arbiter in my heart.
- I claim perfect peace because my mind is fixed on You, the everlasting Rock.
- I thank God that He "disciplines us for our good, that we may share in his holiness." I accept all the bumps and bruises that might bend me out of shape as discipline.
- Instead of someone stuck in a rigid rut that makes me blow up at opposition, "I have become all things to all men" whenever that may help me save some.
- Whatever detours may arise, God will always lead me in triumphal procession in Christ.
- I fall on the Stone and am broken; as a result, I'm not utterly crushed when the rocks of adversity fall on me.

## Sharp Mercy

Let's say your chronic problem is resentment; you need to find a counterpoint virtue for the habit of seething over wrongs done to you or stewing over someone's obnoxious character traits. If the circumstances are right, resentful thoughts can tie you up for hours. What quality can serve as a positive alternative to this handicap?

One incident in Christ's life provides one of the strongest settings imaginable for resentment to dominate. The facts are stark and simple: Christ was nailed to a cross by Roman soldiers. But the emotional implications are enormous. The Messiah lay helpless on the ground as a condemned criminal precisely because the people He had poured His ministry into had turned their backs on Him. The one group that He'd carefully nurtured and taught and forgiven and made great promises to and wooed back from apostasy over thousands of years — these people had screamed in unison for His blood. They stood mocking the climax of their own sacred history.

What an overwhelming opportunity for resentment. Talk about being wronged. Talk about injustice. How could they possibly do this to Him, the desire of all nations, the righteous Branch, the Prince of Peace, the One spelled out in countless sacrifices since Abraham first raised his knife over a spotless lamb?

Jesus should have been seething as the executioners proceeded with their grisly chore, His thoughts choked with bitter recollections. But we don't find a trace of resentment in the innocent victim. Instead we hear an incongruous benediction: "Father forgive them, for they don't know what they're doing." A strong cry of mercy erupts from the bloody ground.

It's one thing to have mercy on the frailty of mankind in general. It's quite another to show mercy to mankind in particular, that calloused piece of humanity which is driving spikes into your limbs. This is unconditional, specific mercy; we might call it the quality of *sharp mercy.* It's not some vague goodwill-toward-men which can be effortlessly celebrated on poster pictures of flowers and cute children. It's a forgiving kindness aimed straight at the heart of the offending party. It's pointed, sharp.

At the cross, Jesus embodied for us a very powerful counterpoint note to the endless drone of resentment. And His sharp mercy rings clear elsewhere in Scripture. So you can re-write another hidden treasure into your mind with the Word:

- Blessed are the merciful, for they shall obtain mercy.
- Love keeps no record of wrongs; it covers a multi-tude of sins.
- God delights to show mercy; He does not treat me as my sins deserve, or repay me according to my iniquities. His sun shines down on the evil and the good; His rain falls on the just and unjust.
- I want to be a part of that mercy that endures for-ever, turns away anger, heals waywardness, and loves freely, the mercy which would spare a city full of depravity for the sake of ten.
- My own transgressions have been thrown into the depths of the sea — how can I keep bringing up someone else's?
- The Omniscient Jehovah vows to remember no more my long string of failures — how can I fume over someone else's?
- My million-dollar deficit has been wiped out by Christ's priceless sacrifice — how can I keep trying to collect on $2.98?

## Resilient Contentment

How about a difficulty that's a little harder to nail down — say the blues. We rarely can pinpoint some act of the will where we let depression come in the door — and I don't think we should regard it as a sin. But it's a problem nevertheless. Can we latch onto some counterpoint virtue? It's particularly important to find an alternative here; depression often becomes quite a convoluted trap—we can get depressed over our depression, depressed by anticipating and remembering it.

If we dissect the blues a bit we generally find some sense of loss at the beginning, followed by a swelling of self-pity, and then a huddling down between grey walls that seem to slowly close in and reinforce the ricochet of gloomy thoughts. A very useful flip-side to this process appears in Paul's statement to the Philippians: "I have learned the secret of being content in any and every situation, whether well fed or hungry, whether living in plenty or in want. I can do everything through him who gives me strength." This statement is especially striking if we recall that Paul was not writing it from the resort beaches of Caesarea, but from imprisonment, probably in Rome, a condition usually designed to inspire terminal depression. In spite of his chains, however, Paul could be content; his emotions did not center around his loss (of freedom, comfort, friends, ministry, sunlight, fresh air) and so he did not feel very sorry for himself.

The secret of Paul's contentment seems to relate to his capacity to "rejoice in the Lord always," that is, to find something to be appreciative about in any situation because of the presence or activity of God. Paul developed a knack for noticing how his Lord worked things out for good in all circumstances, and he also developed a habit of giving thanks in all circumstances. His contentment didn't depend on having a nice day; it went deeper; it was resilient.

That was why Paul, though physically confined, could write such a cheery letter of encouragement to people enjoying life on the outside. He had dug up a hidden treasure: the *resilient contentment* that comes from thankfulness. And that quality left little internal room for depression. In fact, it made self-pity look quite ridiculous when it came knocking at the door looking for a place to get down. As the stoic philosopher Epictetus advised: "Fortify yourself with contentment, for this is an impregnable fortress."

Coming up with thanks under pressure is the new habit that best counters depression. The apostle Peter cues us into such a principle in his first epistle: "But rejoice that you participate in the sufferings of Christ, so that you may be overjoyed when his glory is revealed." The point seems to be that if you manage a knowing smile during the bad times of hurt, you'll be able to truly enjoy the good times of deliverance. Those who find joy even in the gloom will be overjoyed when the clouds roll away. But those who complain now will still be complaining later.

It's a bit like training with weights. After doing squats with two hundred pounds on your back for a while and then dropping the bar to the ground, you feel like you're walking on air. Pushing against the burden of weights is what gives us strength, resilience. But if we just sit around when we're burdened and sink into the couch in self-pity, then even when the weight is removed we'll have become too flabby to take advantage of our freedom; we'll still be plodding along.

Coming up with thanks in adversity is how we turn the burden into a workout. We train, we make positive use of the downward pressure and thus are enabled to really soar later.

So if depression is one of those freeloaders you're trying to get rid of, aim at the resilent contentment which Paul embodied. Get a good picture in your mind of the virtue, the treasure, you are going to pursue. Tell God (remember, don't just talk to yourself):

- I greatly rejoice in my imperishable inheritance.
- I'm receiving a kingdom that can't be shaken.
- I'll offer to my Lord the fruit of my lips, the sacrifice of praise.
- There's always something to be glad about in the Lord; I look at His unfailing love and wonderful deeds on our behalf.
- The Holy Spirit who regenerates and renews has been poured out richly upon me through Jesus Christ; I won't let it go to waste.
- Acknowledging that I'm adorned as a lily, fed as a sparrow, that my Lord withholds nothing good

from me, I overflow with thankfulness and sing spiritual songs with gratitude in my heart.
• I'm resilient in Christ, maybe knocked down, but never out; poor, yet making many rich; having nothing, and yet possessing everything.

This is the picture we need to fix on as we walk out to each day's challenge. Paul's phrase, "overflowing with thankfulness" crystalizes our virtue-objective. We push a flow of thankfulness up against the downward pressure of afflictions small and great. We keep affirming our blessings in Christ until the adversity is removed and our well-exercised spirit of contentment bursts out in a fountain of praise. This is better than self-pity; this is a treasure worth pursuing.

## Acquiring a Skill

Other habits, of course, require other counterpoint virtues. The process of finding those virtues is itself part of the solution; we're already orienting ourselves away from the rut and toward something new. If gossip is the nemesis, study Jesus' life; bore into Scripture and come up with a particular kind of tolerance, one that believes the best and hopes for the best in others. Critical? A nag? Start looking for an alternative—maybe encouragement, the art of edification.

As you begin pursuing a certain virtue, you will hopefully begin to see yourself as acquiring a skill, not just kicking a habit. Don't keep saying, "I'm trying to stop feeling blue." Start saying, "I'm building the skill of contentment." Qualities like solid sensitivity and malleability are not simply quantities of goodness that you try to acquire; they're not points you can rack up; they're special abilities. Skills require practice; we develop them over time as the Holy Spirit does His rewriting; they're fruits of His creative influence.

When we see goodness only as a quantity, then every failure makes us feel we have to go back to square one. We have to tick off a certain number of abstentions in order to get there from here, and every time we stumble it all spills out, the quantity disappears. But when we see our moral goal as a quality, then missteps aren't as likely to send us all the way back. We're practicing; we're trying to acquire a skill. Of course we're going to mess up. But we learn from our mistakes. We bounce back by confessing to and identifying with the crucified Christ and by refocusing on our counterpoint virtue.

Acquiring a skill is a challenge; it can even be fun. Facing a pass/flunk test every day is not. Chronic habits lend themselves to the pass/flunk system — did we do it or not? That's why the quality we're pursuing must dominate: *I'm after hidden treasure. I may stumble, I may fall flat on my face, but I'm still pursuing that quality; it's still my goal. I accept the challenge with gusto.*

Thank God we don't have to be sitting ducks; we're on the move, fleeing youthful lusts (or middle-aged perils) and pursuing after righteousness, faith, love, and peace. We can become women and men for whom God "will fulfill every desire for goodness." Christ's qualities can become more vivid and captivating than the sin that once entangled us.

# 5

# Armed to the Teeth

ONE cool, overcast day beside a Holiday Inn swimming pool I met a man who had wrestled with the hows and whys of chronic sin more earnestly than anyone I'd ever known. In Jack's case the problem was homosexuality. We seated ourselves on the plastic pool-side chairs because that was a quiet place where I could do the interview for a magazine I edited. Jack had founded an organization which counseled gay men desiring to change their sexual orientation. He'd thought long and hard about the dilemmas facing homosexuals; he'd struggled long and hard with the behavior himself. And after years of frustration, Jack finally hit a breakthrough.

I wanted him to spell it out. So for two hours I queried and listened to this very bright and articulate man whose wife and young son were relaxing in their hotel room nearby.

Jack had learned to see gayness not just as a terrifying aberration but as a mistaken attempt to meet a very legitimate need. He'd realized that the homosexual does need satisfying relationships with adult men; many gays require healing because of fathers short on love and affection. Their desires simply need to be re-directed away from sexuality.

Jack said that understanding Jesus as his righteousness, substitute, and surety was a key turning point. Experiencing God's unconditional acceptance helped him escape a self-defeating pattern of behavior which involved denying the problem, then inducing more guilt to keep from sinning, then seeking to eradicate his sinful nature through fasting and desperate prayer.

He felt that temptation had such power over him for so long precisely because it scared him to death; he locked onto it. But Jack finally ceased to regard homosexual feelings as the great enemy of his life, and instead as an instrument to lead him to Christ. Rather than beg God, "Please set me free," he began thanking his Lord that he was free. If he fell into sin, he determined not to let it drag him down, but to go on believing that Christ had given him new life.

My conversation with Jack proved to be very enlightening; here was a man who had dealt with sin on a level that few of us ambling through the Christian life as painlessly as possible ever reach. I had come to respect him enormously. So I was greatly saddened several months later to learn that he had resigned from his position at the ministry. Gay activist groups, in fact, were celebrating his fall. Apparently he had engaged in inappropriate behavior with a young counselee at his center.

Some time afterward, Jack explained. His attempts to provide a young man with a healthy, loving, man-to-man relationship had gone too far. He'd begun to rationalize that his demonstrations of affection were part of therapy and they had progressed into something sexual.

Jack bounced back from his mistake, thank God, and continues to have a great relationship with his wife, although it has been more difficult to build back credibility in the wider world.

### Come Out Swinging

It is of course impossible for someone on the outside to pinpoint the reason for Jack's lapse. But mulling over his experience, I came to a conclusion significant for my own struggle with habits: It's possible to be too positive in dealing with sin. Jack had been burned so badly by his protracted loathing of the sin that he wanted to see only good. He had resisted for so long with such a sense of failure that he wanted to stop fighting and simply claim victory. I respected Jack for all this; we do need to aim at the virtue, not at the temptation. But if there was a weakness in his strategy, it was the lack of a resolve to identify a wrong when it showed up and turn sharply away from it. He tried very hard to transform every pull toward the old life into something that could be legitimately fulfilled — in a slightly revised context.

All this has value. It took Jack a long way, and still does, I believe. But it apparently created as a side-effect that spot of vulnerability. He was not ready soon enough to give an unequivocal *no*.

A battle strategy of zeroing in on sin is a big mistake. But it's possible to fall off the other side of the horse, too: zeroing in on our new identity, our virtue, our positive potential, to the point where we don't even confront sin. We want to completely ignore the problem, and so when it does break through in our face we're not prepared to fight. In the last chapter we tried to set our aim on a counterpoint virtue to prevent sin from dominating our horizon. But now we also need a measure of belligerence, a willingness to kick out that offensive party.

### Witness for the Prosecution

The first problem we need to overcome as we step out from our quiet time into the day's activities is a tendency toward timidity. We need to affirm in very strong terms that our virtue wins hands down over whatever temptation may come to challenge it. Too often we retain a ducking-our-head posture as we scurry out into the secular traffic of the big bad world. It's easy to be intimidated and accused because of our obvious history of failure.

So it's time to take a stance as accusers ourselves in God's name. We can search out, meditate on, and internalize Scripture which turns us into witnesses for the prosecution — always in terms of showing that God's character quality (which we're aiming at) stands as a rebuke to its opposite evil number.

I remember one gloomy day when I was trying to crawl out from under yet another defeat at the hands of my old habit; it had been one of those pre-meditated, deliberate falls. Everything was blurry; I wanted to acknowledge before God that I had done wrong, to agree with Him in confession, but the sin had become so familiar that it was difficult to make any statement that didn't ring hollow. Even more, I badly wanted some way to meaningfully express repentance, to feel repentance. I was pretty numb, and I knew that the future good fight of faith required me to find some handle for the will, some inspiration for resistance.

So I kept praying, and I laid out my jaded soul before the Lord, asking for help. Then I began perusing the Scriptures for something that might nourish me awake. My eyes fell on Luke's account of Pilate caught between an innocent Jesus and an angry mob. The Roman could get no answer to his repeated question, "What crime has He committed?" The crowd just kept chanting, "Crucify Him! Crucify Him!" Pilate suggested a half-way measure: How about if we give the Nazarene a good whipping and then let Him go? The mob was in no mood for compromise: "But they were urgent, demanding with loud cries that He should be crucified. And their voices prevailed."

That last sentence fell on me like lead. "Their voices prevailed." That was what had just happened to me. Temptation had been urgent, demanding and loud in my head, the chant of the carnal nature. And I knew exactly what it required of me: to deny the lordship of Jesus over this sexual area of my life (temporarily of course). I had to turn my back on Him. Yes, the same ugly shout had prevailed over me, too.

Needless to say, I found a handle for inspired repentance. But more than that, I found a personal battle cry. The next time that urgent voice of temptation slid into the seat beside me,

I would hear the echo of a bloodthirsty mob, "Crucify Him!" Did I want their shouts to become the last word?

"Their voices prevailed" (a bit like "Remember the Alamo") — those words helped me overcome a tendency to go limp whenever temptation bullied. The phrase helped me become instead a witness against sin, a witness for the prosecution: *You are the voice that seeks to crucify Christ. I accuse you in His name; be silent.*

Later I would find and learn to value other verses and other battle cries. This needs to be a continuing process of discovery and application. We set the stage for overcoming the evil one by witnessing against him; we're able to expose him and his lies:

- You want me to be the dog returning to its vomit, the washed sow who goes back to wallowing in the mud. You want to put an iron yoke around my neck until I am destroyed. You want to turn this temple (of the Holy Spirit) into some den of robbers.
- You exile people to an outer darkness where there will be weeping and gnashing of teeth.
- I refuse to be hardened by the deceitfulness of sin. I will not suppress God's truth by this wickedness; I will not serve some created thing rather than the Creator or become an adversary of the cross of Christ or turn my stomach into a god.
- I refuse to drop into the trap of the devil who takes people captive to do his will.
- I identify with faithful Joseph alone in an alien culture who, when pressed by temptation, bore witness: "How can I do this great wickedness and sin against God?" I identify with Daniel, isolated in a foreign world, who "resolved not to defile himself with the royal food and wine."

Find verses that raise the battle cry in your own mind. Take a stance as active witness, joining your voice with that of a youthful David whose spunky faith cried out, "You may come against me with an assortment of weapons but I come against you in the name of the Lord Almighty, the God of the armies of Israel, whom you have defied."

The tug of sin is an affront to the living God; stand up for His Name, become a witness for the prosecution.

## A Choir in Combat

In our endeavor to stay on the offensive, a healthy balance is required — we don't go out looking for a fight, but if it comes, we're prepared to come out swinging. The trick is to arm ourselves without losing our original focus on where we do want to go. We need to be prepared to oppose evil, and yet not center on temptation or sin. How do we do that? The classic answer is provided by King Jehoshaphat and the people of Judah in one of their brightest moments (see 2 Chronicles 20). A vast army of Moabites and Ammonites was marching straight toward Jerusalem. In response to this terrifying invasion, the king turned his attention, and that of his people, to the "God of our fathers," declaring in prayer: "You rule over all the kingdoms. . . . Power and might are in Your hand, and no one can withstand You."

Afterward, the men of Judah strode out in battle array to intercept their enemies at the Pass of Ziz. However, heading this army was not a squad of the strongest warriors, but a choir singing about the splendor of Yahweh's holiness. The Hebrews' counterattack became a religious procession, loudly proclaiming: "Give thanks to the Lord, for His love endures forever."

As this stream of praise neared the invading horde, the Moabites and Ammonites inexplicably began fighting among themselves. By the time the choir arrived at an overlook, they saw nothing but dead bodies stretched out over the Desert of Jeruel.

Note that the Israelites did not just sit tight in Jerusalem and try to ignore the rumble of marching feet; they went out to confront the enemy. But they also did not focus on all those well-armed adversaries; they led with their greatest weapon: the holy, loving and powerful El Shaddai.

The key to victory is simply to concentrate on our weapons as opposed to simply our enemy. Our arsenal should loom larger than the sin. Fight yes, scared no.

# Holy Trinity & Co.

The Word of God is presented to us by Paul as the sword of the Spirit, a formidable, offensive weapon. We may wield Scripture to great effect, as Jesus did in His weakest moment, harassed by Satan out in the Judean desert. Our Lord cut the enemy down very neatly and devastatingly with the Word. It is more than just a tool for fending off assaults, it is "living and active," piercing to the marrow as a double-edged sword.

This "sword of the Spirit" is powerful principally because it is a means of activating all our other resources; it places many other weapons at our disposal. Here's a brief look at our arsenal.

### The Warrior God

First of all, we have none other than King Yahweh who presents Himself as a great warrior fighting on our behalf. In the psalms we find a God who straps a sword to His thigh, rides to victory as a splendid fighter, and marches through Zion's gates a conquering hero, mighty in battle. He even takes on Leviathan, the embodiment of all that terrified the ancients, and crushes its head in the sea.

The prophet Zephaniah shows us God as enthusiastic rescuer: "The Lord your God is in your midst. A victorious warrior. He will exult over you with joy. . . ."

This El Shaddai is aroused to snatch us from the jaws of the tyrant. He prevails over all opponents, taking on evil powers, rulers, and gods in order to expose their inadequacies and shatter their presumptuous claims. The warrior God overpowers rivals; He forces them into situations where, like blind and dumb idols, they cannot perform. Jehovah is out there leading the charge; we don't have to slink into battle.

Soon after a St. Louis lawyer named Scofield accepted Christ as Savior, he found himself trembling before the inevitable battle with old habits: "The one thing I was in mortal fear of was that I might go back to my sins. I [had] no power over an appetite for strong drink." Scofield did his best at avoidance — crossing the street whenever he came near a tavern. But his defensive struggle was quickly burning him out. "I was in torment day and night. No one had told me anything about the keeping power of Jesus Christ." He felt he had no potent spiritual weapons at his disposal.

But then, a week after his conversion, he passed by the large show window of a store which sold paintings. An engraving displayed there caught his eye; it pictured Daniel in the den of lions. As the beasts circled around the prophet, Daniel looked up to answer King Darius's anxious question, "Has your God been able to rescue you?"

Suddenly Scofield saw himself in the painting: "These lions are all about me — my old habits and sins." But the prophet was standing there calm, confident, and unharmed. The mighty God of heaven had shut the lion's mouths. Scofield was struck by a new, powerful picture of the God he had chosen to follow. He was the Deliverer; strong enough to stifle the passions of ravenous lions. "He had saved me, and He was able to deliver me from the lions. Oh what a rest it was!"

A bracing look at our Warrior God, as opposed to fearful glances at our besetting sin, turns withering struggles into good fights.

**The Blood of Christ**

The cross stands as ground zero of our thermonuclear response to sin. It is the great dividing blast which can make the world dead to me and me dead to the world. The blood of Christ makes demons tremble; the most confident sins go limp when pressed by this sacrifice. If called upon in earnest, the spotless Lamb becomes the roaring Lion of Judah and turns the bellow of Satan into a whimper.

Jesus on Golgotha is a great heroic spectacle to have on our side; a good look at Christ crucified can overwhelm even the flashing neural neon of the most persistent temptations. We are assured by the Word that Jesus lifted up on the cross will draw us unfailingly to Himself, that the blood of Christ can purge our consciences of those "dead works" still loitering within, and that the manifestation of this divine sacrifice puts away sin and rescues us from the present evil age. Even in the heat of the Apocalyspe, believers are said to overcome the Accuser "by the blood of the Lamb."

Martin Luther was once asked how he dealt with the assaults of the devil. The reformer replied, "Well, when he comes knocking upon the door of my heart, and asks 'Who lives here?' the dear Lord Jesus goes to the door and says, 'Martin Luther used to live here but he has moved out. Now I live here.' The devil, seeing the nail-prints in the hands, and the pierced side, takes flight immediately."

When the old habit comes knocking, send Jesus to the door.

## Spirit's Power

God the Holy Spirit presents Himself to us as a weapon also, primarily through His ability to "strengthen us with power in the inner man." He is the energizer. If the Word of God is a sword in our hands, then the Holy Spirit is the impulse and resilient strength to wield it. Romans 8 highlights this life-giving Spirit as the power which enables our spiritual death to become spiritual resurrection. Zechariah's classic battle cry: "Not by might nor by power, but by my Spirit, says the Lord Almighty," implies that mere physical force or military strength is no match for the enabling power of the Spirit.

Some have had quite close encounters with this God of the Interior. Charles Finney seems to have been driven straight into Him one day after he was suddenly moved to "pour my whole soul out to God" in intense prayer for some time. He recalled, "The Holy Spirit descended upon me in a manner that seemed to go through me, body and soul. I could feel the impression, like a wave of electricity, going through and through me. Indeed, it seemed to come in waves and waves of liquid love. . . . I can recollect distinctly that it seemed to fan me, like immense wings." These "waves of love" continued pouring over the awestruck man until he cried out, "Lord, I cannot bear any more."

Very few of us will ever be bowled over by the Spirit in the way this remarkable frontier evangelist was. But through such people we do get a glimpse of the Spirit as a powerful force in human life. His potential is indeed awesome. If we fear the old temptation breaking over us in waves, remember that the Spirit can do likewise. If we just give Christ a good, hard look, pouring out our heart, we'll catch some of the power that overwhelmed Finney.

This is how the Holy Trinity itself stands as an arsenal awaiting whatever poor temptation may be unlucky enough to pass by. Of course it's important to refrain from reducing the Godhead to some magical tool in our hands. God, in His fullness, is a weapon only because He is willing to minister to us in certain ways: as Victorious Warrior, as Blood Sacrifice, as Inner Power. These are aspects of His many-faceted person which we may call on and claim in order to become instruments ourselves in the good fight of faith.

## Angelic Hosts

A servant of the prophet Elisha woke up one morning and looked out on a terrifying sight. From the walls of Dothan, the man saw an entire army camped in a circle around the city. The King of Aram had slipped up with his troops in the night and laid a trap for Elisha, whom he believed was providing the king of Israel with valuable intelligence.

Elisha's servant looked out on infantry, cavalry and charioteers — all armed to the teeth and spread out over the hills surrounding Dotham. He began trembling; there seemed no possible way of escape. Running to his master, Elisha, he exclaimed, almost in a panic, "Oh, my lord, what shall we do?"

The prophet remained strangely calm and replied with these remarkable words: "Don't be afraid. Those who are with us are more than those who are with them."

The servant didn't quite understand. Surely the handful of Dotham residents who could bear arms were no match for this invading army! Elisha read his servant's fear and perplexity and asked God to open the man's eyes so he could see a picture more real than all the assembled troops of King Aram.

God responded. The servant's eyes were opened wider than he could imagine; suddenly, he saw another army out there. The besiegers were themselves surrounded by a host of angels whose horses and chariots of fire covered the hills. It was true, the forces allied with the prophet Elisha were far greater than those supporting the invading king.

We need to keep our eyes opened wide today. It's easy to see only the threats against us out there or only a barren sky swept clean of angelic hosts. But God guarantees us the weapon of angels. They constantly proceed from His throne on errands of rescue. So we must continually acknowledge that those standing on our side are greater than any taunting gang the enemy can muster. We may with confidence call on those servants called "winds" and "flames of fire," those formidable allies, because:

". . .he will command his angels concerning you
>to guard you in all your ways;
>they will lift you up in their hands,
>>so that you will not strike your foot
>>>against a stone" (Psalm 91:11–12).

## Don't Duel, Overwhelm

With the Trinity & Company aligned behind us, we must be prepared to strike swift and sure blows against the enemy, as opposed to sitting down and having a chat with him. Being armed to the teeth is similar in a way to adversary empires stockpiling nuclear weapons. The threat is what counts; you want to avoid at all costs getting into a heated confrontation which will force you to toss missiles back and forth.

If we wait until temptation is breathing down our necks and about to push us under before we think about our weapons, then we'll be forced into a very perilous stance in combat. We don't want to get into a protracted argument with the world, the flesh, or the devil over the merits of some sin. We don't want to hang around the bargaining table. We simply want to show up armed to the teeth, prepared to overwhelm temptation.

Here's what usually happens when the old temptation comes knocking again. First it simply drifts by and waves a polite greeting. You give a look, then grimace and turn away. After a bit it drifts by a little more slowly and smiles. You shake your head and turn to other things. The temptation may make several passes at you during the day, and each time that smile sinks in a bit deeper—even though you're still shaking your head.

Purely passive resistance puts you at a disadvantage, particularly if the temptation extends over time. Those sinful suggestions leave an impression in the mind, a subconscious imprint that can weaken resolve. So when the old enemy decides to stop drifting and plops down right in front of your face, you find yourself surprisingly easy prey. When the battle between sin and non-sin bursts out in black and white, you finally try to whip out some weapons. But you've already conceded too much ground—thinking how nice it would be to give in—and you tend to fire stepping backwards.

The best defense is a good offense. We can overwhelm temptation if we attack it at the first drift. That's our golden opportunity. The first little lurid suggestion, the first appearance of the enemy, should call forth an artillery barrage, not just a warning shot from the hip. Heap Scripture on this temptation that dares to defy the Living God.

- I know that, "Thy right hand, O Lord, glorious in power, Thy right hand, O Lord, shatters the enemy."

- Does a vast army of Egyptians threaten me? God has "put darkness between me and the Egyptians and made the sea come upon them and cover them."
- I affirm Paul's proclamation: "We destroy . . . every proud obstacle to the knowledge of God and take every thought captive to obey Christ."
- I see the Almighty whispering encouragement to the prophet Jeremiah under siege by his morally watered-down compatriots: "To withstand them I will make you impregnable, a wall of bronze. They will attack you, but they will not prevail, for I am with you to deliver you and save you, says the Lord."

This is how we deny the devil a foothold and how we make him flee: by making a pre-emptive strike against his assaults. We overwhelm the first sign of temptation with our arsenal; we don't just try to persuade it to leave us alone.

Again, resisting the evil one calls for a conscious balance. We must never lose sight of that hidden treasure we're after; it's in pursuing virtue that we are compelled to kick out temptation. We don't go out looking for a fight, but if the enemy does make an appearance we are prepared to beat him to a pulp.

During the Revolutionary War, an Irishman in the American service came upon a small party of Hessians in the woods foraging for food. He quickly seized their arms, which they'd laid aside, and pointed his musket at his shocked adversaries. Making loud threats, the Irishman managed to drive them back to the American camp. His entrance caused some wonder. Brought with the prisoners before General Washington, he was asked how he'd singlehandedly taken these professional mercenaries. "By God, general," he replied, "I surrounded them."

You may feel quite alone in trying to point your weapons at habitual enemies who seem much more adept at fighting. But always remember that with God, the Mighty Warrior, Crucified Son, and Powerful Spirit, you do have them quite surrounded.

# 6

# Expressed in Action

DURING China's protracted conflict between feudal lords, known as the time of the Warring States, the area of Fan-Shih was subjugated by Chih-Pai. An enterprising citizen from the latter city-state managed to steal a prized bell from Fan-Shih as his own private tribute. The man slipped it in a sack, slung it over his shoulder, and attempted to walk casually through the streets, unnoticed. But as he instinctively hurried his pace, the bell rang out a sharp and penetrating "ding dong." The thief reflexively put his hands over his ears, shutting out the telltale sound, and imagining in that split second that the rest of the world would go deafly about its business as well.

We're now armed to the teeth and aiming at a virtue; it's time to act. We must do something with that bell from the enemy camp that has rung defiantly over us for so long. The good fight mustn't remain confined to our minds; it has to be realized in behavior.

Unfortunately, again, we struggling believers often wind up with negative action on our hands—we merely avoid doing this, keep from falling into that. Our first reaction to embarassing habits is often something similar to the thief covering his ears. We try to do something that shuts out the ringing, that turns off the symptoms. But non-sin does not bring the same rewards or the same reinforcement as actually *doing the law.* What we need are positive, counterpoint actions which give expression to our counterpoint virtue. That telltale ringing won't really stop until we replace the bell. We know we have this weakness, what we need is behavior which replaces it. Christian Counselor Jay Adams relates this to the putting off of the old man and the putting on of the new man described in Ephesians 4.

### Down in Black and White

First try to break down your chronic problem into specific behavior. What exactly are you doing that makes you say you often get depressed or have a bad temper or struggle with resentment? Sometimes the behavior will be obvious: When things go wrong you kick the door, pound on the table, swear, or yell at the kids. Yes, you have a problem with uncontrolled anger.

At other times you may have to look more carefully. Say you put down your wife a lot. Ask when, where, how. Nail this problem on the head. You complain about her cooking in front of guests, or make her feel stupid by belaboring her mistakes, or brush off her questions as trivial by answering curtly. Get it down in black and white.

Sometimes the behavior will seem exclusively mental or emotional. You just resent so-and-so, that's it; you stew about him or her. In this case try to identify what you do as a result of your negative emotion. How do you treat the one resented? Cold shoulder, cool civility, gossip, small acts of revenge?

Or say your problem is the blues—you just feel bad, that's all. Well, what happens when you get depressed? Do you sleep all the time, mope around the house, whine at your spouse, review your sorry lot in life over and over?

Analyzing our problem in terms of particular actions helps us be more honest with God and ourselves. That human heart, "more deceitful than all else" and "desperately sick," tends to camouflage its most serious problems and tone down conviction into something general and abstract. We need to see exactly what we're doing.

It may also be useful to gauge the frequency of our problem behavior. This helps especially if it's something we slip into over and over subconsciously, or if we've underestimated the seriousness of our habit, as so often happens. A good measure of frequency over a period of time can serve as a baseline with which to check on future progress. So try keeping a record of your behavior each day for a week, and note when, how often, and under what circumstances you fall into the old pattern.

All this, however, should not lead us into some kind of groveling exercise where we make ourselves miserable over all those painful misdeeds which seem to blanket our week with transgression. We just want a quick, accurate diagnosis—all the while remaining under the care of the Great Physician who accepts us unconditionally.

### Counterpoint Behavior

Now we're ready to move on to the next step: breaking down our counterpoint virtue into concrete counterpoint behavior. We want to express our hidden treasure by deeds which replace our chronic sin. It's best if we zero in on actions which overwhelm the habit, not just compete with it. That is, if we're doing X, we can't be doing Y at the same time. This is known in psychology textbook terms as "simultaneous and incompatible" behavior, actions which exclude their opposite number.

Paul, for example, suggests this healthy alternative for habitual thieves: "He who has been stealing must steal no longer, but must work, doing something useful with his own hands, that he may have something to share with those in need"

(Ephesians 4:28). Stealing from others and working to share with the needy are psychologically incompatible. Elsewhere in Scripture, believers are urged to replace falsehood with speaking the truth, drunkenness with singing in the Spirit, and trading insults with bestowing blessings. Notice that even the ethic of non-violence is not treated as a passive non-sin by Jesus. He tells us to replace hitting back with turning the other cheek.

Let's look at a few positive, counterpoint actions.

### Malleability — Acts of Thanksgiving

Say you've selected the quality of being malleable before God as your goal. How can you demonstrate that virtue in ways that exclude the problem behavior you've identified? Perhaps you most commonly blow up when a physical object frustrates your efforts — the vacuum cleaner won't work, the oil nut won't budge, the bicycle tire tube won't come out — and you most commonly vent anger by swearing and pounding on the stubborn thing (embarassing yourself in front of your children; it's pretty bad when your five-year-old has to have a heart-to-heart talk with Daddy about his language).

What can you *do* to express malleability in those situations? How about thanking God for this present obstacle? We know that He uses trials as a means to help us grow and that He desires all circumstances to work out for some good, so we have plenty of reasons to give thanks. This action declares that we choose to be malleable and not rigid. And it also excludes our problem behavior; it's pretty hard to swear and kick the lawn mower when you are thanking God — simultaneously incompatible.

So this could be our goal: At the first sign of frustration, we'll stop, pause in our work, look up, and speak thanks to our Lord for this problem and His willingness to make something good come out of it. John Ruskin wrote: "There's no music in a 'rest,' but there's the making of music in it. And people are always missing that part of the life melody. . . ." Thanksgiving is the music we put into the "rest" of malleability.

We probably won't get it right the first few times; we'll blow up right away and remember to thank God later. Just stop at whatever point you find yourself and give thanks. If you maintain your daily aim at malleability in prayer and keep in touch with the Word which illuminates that quality, you will find yourself stopping earlier and earlier in your anger. Keep praying about malleability and claiming it as your personal goal; don't just pray about your failure.

With thanks comes a little perspective. You don't take yourself (or the stupid vacuum cleaner) quite so seriously. You start smiling more as you give thanks, seeing humor in your predicament rather than just an enemy who must be crushed.

### Sharp Mercy — Intercessory Prayer

Then there's resentment. Say the problem behavior you've nailed down is repeating Sandy's obnoxious qualities over and over in your mind every time you see her at the office. She just sets off a welter of ugly thoughts. If you've taken good aim at the quality of sharp mercy, how can you give it concrete expression?

Try the positive, counterpoint action of praying for Sandy. First find some legitimate need she has which you can petition God about. (It's best if this does not relate directly to the trait that drives you up the wall; focusing on that could turn prayer into another gripe session.) Then, at the first sign of seething over Sandy, stop, recall her needs, and pray to God about them. Again, you may not stop early enough the first few times. Just keep your aim on sharp mercy and keep stopping at whatever point you can. You will find it impossible to pray for Sandy and resent her at the same time.

In college I became involved with an "action group" in Campus Crusade for Christ. It was a new experience for me; I'd never known religion could be so vital to my contemporaries. During our weekly fellowship sessions we five guys developed a very supportive closeness.

But one evening, a six-foot-five football player burst into our quiet gathering, extended his hand in all directions, and bellowed out his name. Big Wally, I discovered, was the latest addition to our group. For me the spell was broken; I was sure our meetings would never be the same. This primitive extrovert had ruined our tranquil, reflective atmosphere.

As I listened to Wally's opinions boom across the room during subsequent sessions, I realized that not only were our personalities poles apart, but many of his all-American religious views were those I disdained.

Fortunately, our group leader came up with a new way to open our fellowship time. He asked us to pray silently for each group member, thinking of their needs and claiming God's assistance in their lives. I prayed for the person on my right, on my left, then came to Wally, sitting across the room. Somehow I could no longer think of him in the same way. He required my help, and I his.

The act of blessing jolted me into a different perspective, and I began to see things I admired in the effusive jock. The more we prayed together, the more I came to like Wally, until one evening I found myself jumping on a sofa with him, wildly celebrating an answer to prayer. His raw enthusiasm had become infectious rather than offensive.

Praying for our resentee doesn't always transform a relationship so dramatically. But it does pry open a loophole in an otherwise open-and-shut case of animosity. When we pray, we are all needy children before the Father. And when we know a person has needs, he can no longer be an enemy.

### Solid Sensitivity — Compliments

How about the old nemesis of lust? You realize that you've been locking on the attributes of every attractive man or woman who walks by and getting lost in adulterous fantasies. You want to have solid sensitivity instead. How do you express it?

Try this. Begin selecting people of the opposite sex you see regularly who are *not* sexually attractive to you — the ones you tend to ignore. Look for something about them that you can admire, some inner quality, a special way they have of doing things. Then give them a word of encouragement about this admirable trait. Long ago a courtier managed this even amid the stilted atmosphere of French court life. He said of a certain Madame de Stael, who lacked physical attraction but was a great conversationalist, that she "had the power of talking herself into a beauty."

You don't have to try to rack up a compliment a day and turn this into an artificial exchange. But make sure you keep looking for something to esteem in a person who normally wouldn't catch your eye. As you begin expressing solid sensitivity concretely, it will become more and more real in your mind; the abstraction turns into tangible hidden treasure. And soon you will find yourself picking up on inner qualities in attractive people, as well.

One woman used this counterpoint behavior to replace a different problem: nagging her spouse. Anya Bateman decided she would give husband Val at least one sincere compliment every day for three weeks. Her criticism had become a habitual reaction: "It seemed as if I couldn't help myself." But Anya reasoned that surely she could find one thing to admire about Val each day. At first her efforts were a bit awkward; she still noticed all the bad things and had to consciously look for something positive. Although Anya felt like a phony at times, she persisted. Soon she began finding more and more nice things to say about the man she'd married, and Val himself became more warmly responsive. At the end of the three weeks, she was amazed at how easy and natural praise had become. "It's a terrific feeling!" she concluded, having replaced a habit and in the process revitalized her marriage.

## Contentment — Thanksgiving

Perhaps it's the blues that get you on a regular basis and you're trying to take good aim at resilient contentment. How do you express that quality? How about making a list each day of ten things you're thankful for? You may have to look hard, but determine to find them. If you have toddlers, listen to them pray; they'll show you things to be thankful for that you've probably ignored. Get your blessings down in black and white; memorize the list if necessary. Perhaps you can turn it into a psalm which you pray to God. Establish that island of contentment in the midst of your blues, and watch it grow.

The habit we're dealing with here is simply moodiness, self-pity, feeling down. If your depression arises from serious emotional traumas or becomes so deep that you are completely debilitated, then you probably need professional help. But for the periodic blues, adopt a positive, counterpoint behavior. Make a list; act on the hidden treasure of contentment. You can't feel sorry for yourself and give thanks at the same time.

## Doable Steps

Whatever the habit that troubles you, the law of God is deep and wide enough to replace it; there are plenty of counterpoint behaviors in Scripture waiting to be adopted. This is the basic training which Paul talked about in 1 Corinthians 9, "I buffet my body and make it my slave." It's disciplined training in righteousness. Your specific, counterpoint behavior can become an effective alternative to the old habit, and may just blossom into a great gift.

It's important, however, to break down that desired behavior into small, doable steps. If you find yourself failing all the time, just aim at a smaller step. Eloquent intercessory prayer for obnoxious Susan won't flow out of you very easily at first. Just a quick plea heavenward whenever you start your resentment routine can serve as your initial goal. Then work to make your steps a bit bigger, progressing from upward groans to real prayer to real insights into her needs.

# What Triggers the Habit

## Checking Out Antecedents

If you still find yourself slipping into your habit before you can begin to express a counterpoint virtue, there's something else you can do.

As you start aiming at a specific behavioral goal, it often helps to look carefully at exactly what leads up to the behavior you're trying to replace. Take a good look at when, where, and how you fall into that chronic sin. This is known as analyzing the "antecedents." You may discover certain cues that frequently precede your problem behavior and seem to trigger it. Antecedents are the tools our carnal nature uses to pry us into transgression.

Perhaps a lack of sleep or surfeit of time on your hands usually preceed your blues. Watching certain television shows or videos may relate to periods of adulterous fantasy. Criticism from your spouse could be the factor that triggers your resentment of someone else. Try to step back and look at the larger picture; what is the environment of your habit? Are outbursts of anger in the tool shed related to stress at the office? Do certain windowed envelopes in the mail often precede your overdosing on worry?

Sometimes our initial effort to nail down our problem in terms of specific behavior will automatically highlight antecedents. We see precisely when, where, and how we misbehave. At other times our habits come with more complicated connections and we must dig a bit to find the cues. It's important to become aware of more than just isolated wrongful acts. Part of the godly wisdom advertised in the book of Proverbs involves disciplined alertness: "The prudent see danger and take refuge, but the simple keep going and suffer for it."

The New Testament advises us to "leave no loop-hole for the devil" and to "make no provision for the flesh."

## Removing Bad Cues

What we do with antecedents once we find them depends on the nature of the beast. Some require the basic preventative prudence that Proverbs commends. We have to avoid certain things that trigger transgression. If certain types of movies pave the way for lustful thoughts, then they have to go. You may have to avoid certain places that major in seductive images. If you're fighting fat, then the street lined with pastry shops is the wrong place to go for a walk; you may have to avoid altogether that store with the luscious ice cream flavors displayed right by the check-out counter. These kinds of overwhelming antecedents are the enemy's ground; they pre-sell us on the habit. Seeing danger from a distance is the key here; that's what prudence means. Any fool can acknowledge it when it stares him in the face, but by then it's usually too late.

And sometimes of course we *want* it to stare us in the face. We're like the boy on the way to a ballpark whose mother forbade him to swim in a pond enroute. He decided to take along his bathing suit, "just in case I get tempted."

## Early-Warning System

But at times we can't avoid danger. We'll probably be assailed by food for lust or food for obesity at some point in our day's activities. We can't get rid of all stress in our lives. Things will happen to get us mad, either on the freeway, at the office, or at home. Identifying antecedents shouldn't become a way to come up with excuses. There's always something that nudges us into sin. It's what we do with those nudges that creates our character as human beings.

So what can we do with unavoidable antecedents which drive us straight to the habit? Use them as an early-warning system. We simply move our strategy up; we cue into our positive, counterpoint behavior earlier. For example, we don't wait until we're surrounded by prurient images (inside and out) before beginning to look around for some inner quality to compliment. We start that process when we see the first sign of danger. Or if stress at the office paves the way for angry outbursts at our family, we move the practice of malleability up. We stop, give thanks, and smile at ourselves at the first sign of pressure building.

Our counterpoint virtue can replace many negative antecedents just as it does negative behavior. In fact it's better that way, far easier to overwhelm a habit at the root than during a growth spurt.

Other kinds of antecedents don't aim directly at sin; they are problems which can be solved rather than just temptations to avoid. If a lack of sleep contributes to depression, that problem can be solved. If eating a lot of junk food preceeds your edgy nerves, that problem should be solved.

There are also antecedents which, when exposed, prove to be the major problem and show that the original habit is more of a symptom. Perhaps your blues are usually preceeded by some irate outburst about irritant X. Uncontrolled anger may be the behavior you need to replace. Or perhaps your resentment of co-workers is a way to deal with criticism from your spouse. Improving your marital relationship may be the key to your getting along with others better. If your spouse does have a serious habit of putting you down, then that needs to be dealt with, in counseling if necessary. If you are simply unable to take any kind of criticism, then that is the primary behavior to deal with; aim at a counterpoint virtue that relates to this defensiveness.

## The Key Antecedent

In talking about the context of our habits, we should note there is one antecedent more compelling than all the others put together. That is the quality of time spent in Bible study and prayer. Our devotions have more potential to influence behavior than all the triggers and cues and stimuli we can dig up around our habit. If we have a good time of communication with God in the morning, our chances of success that day are much greater than if we get all the techniques down right but just give Him a short, obligatory greeting after getting out of bed. Every strategy recommended in these chapters is worked out only by spending prayerful time in the Word in search of battle cries, a new identity, counterpoint virtues, and so on.

The direct relationship between quality quiet time and healthy growth is something that's been pounded into me over and over again. When it comes to practical spirituality, most of us are painfully slow learners. But I've clearly seen that as soon as my devotions slip-slide away, my good fight of faith turns into a disorderly retreat. A few years ago the Lord took pains to draw that point in billboard-size letters for my benefit.

I had arranged to film a Norwegian medical student jogging in the hills near his Southern California university very early one morning in order to catch him against the sunrise. Sigve's conversion story included a lot of involvement in athletics, and I wanted to picture that as he spoke. We met just as the sun was peeking over mountains to the east. Usually I prayed with those involved before filming, but that day we were in a hurry, not wanting to lose a minute of those precious near-horizontal golden rays.

I had mapped out his course over some hillocks, and Sigve took off. Things went beautifully; rising up and down rhythmically in the camera frame with the sun blazing behind him, I got every angle, plenty of movement toward the camera and across the horizon—everything I needed for a good edit. The ambiance couldn't be beat.

Finally we stopped; Sigve stood catching his breath and I stared at the camera wanting to make sure I had captured every shot possible and exploited this gorgeous sunrise to the max. It was then that a horrible premonition of doom swept over me; something looked funny. I opened up the camera and found it empty, no film cartridge. Incredible.

Everything we'd done that morning added up to one big fat zero. After groaning a great deal, I persuaded a very understanding Sigve to go through his paces again. But of course the magic was gone. The perfect sunrise had turned into just another smoggy morning.

In wondering how I could have made such a pathetically stupid mistake, something which had never happened before, I remembered that in our quite legitimate hurry we had skipped our prayer that day. That sank in. I didn't think that God was punishing me for neglecting some ritual act which magically opened the door for His blessing. But I did think I had just been hit between the eyes by an object lesson—one that the Lord wanted to make sure I grasped at the beginning of my career.

We may be extremely busy. We may have very legitimate needs to care for, including those of our family. But if we don't somehow make regular time for a devotional life, then we're running on empty—there's no film in the camera. We can go through the right motions over and over again but still remain in the same spot where we started with our habit.

## Asking for a Rendezvous

Our daily devotions, as well as being the most significant antecedent around, can also become a time to take aim at other antecedents and turn them into a rendezvous with God. Here's how it works.

Let's say your problem is resentment and you've decided that sharp mercy requires you to look for some deeper need in obnoxious Susan. In your morning devotions ask God to show you one: "Today jog my mind, Lord; help me see what You want for this person; make it clear and make it sink in." Continue to make that request until something happens.

In this way you are asking God to be an antecedent, to give you some sign that prods you into praying for the person you've been stuck resenting. Then, when some insight about Susan comes (maybe even a revelation that didn't seem possible before), you gain an exhilarating sense that God is very much with you. You've made a connection with Him during the day, a rendezvous, and that inspires you all the more to act in sharp mercy.

You can do something very similar if you're trying to un-cover an admirable quality in a person of the opposite sex who normally wouldn't catch your eye. In the morning pray for a rendezvous: "Lord, today please show me a quality to value in Joe. I pray he'll act in some way that catches my new eye of solid sensitivity." You keep praying and wait for the connec-tion. Expect to respond to the promptings of the Holy Spirit. Suddenly you notice something about Joe's routine tasks at the office; you see an admirable quality and feel that God is press-ing it home. This, again, can be inspiration that moves you to express the chosen virtue.

Praying for a rendezvous enables us to glimpse a God who acts with us. It's one thing to give mental assent to the idea that the Lord is involved in our efforts to be good, quite an-other to see Him actively cooperating, making the connection. Seeing (not just acknowledging) that God is involved in a certain specific goal powerfully motivates us. It provides the interruption in our routine that can rescue us. We all don't maintain a meditative, God-oriented mind throughout the day, ready to spring into holy action. We have to function at work or school or home; there are things to do. And in that process it's easy to forget about our goal until unfortunate antecedents have pushed us into sin. Asking for a rendezvous means ask-ing for an interruption: *Remind me, Lord. Put up a sign I can see. Meet me somewhere today.*

Making such a connection is a skill that must be devel-oped through trial and error. It's possible to fall into an unhealthy expectation of arbitrary signs from God — *If You want me to like Susan, make us get stuck in the elevator together.* It's possible to start making signs a condition of your expressing a certain virtue: "Well, God didn't bowl me over with a rev-elation about Susan; I have no choice but to keep on resenting her." We must be persistent in asking for God's intervention only because we remain persistent in aiming at our goal.

Just remember that there's plenty of room for experiment, plenty of possible rendezvous. If anger is tripping you up and you're trying to thank God when you can't get the oil filter off, ask in the morning for a meeting: "Please interrupt me when I start working on the car; show me something about Your craftsmanship through that piece of machinery." If depression is the big adversary and you're trying to make a list of thanksgiving, ask for a meeting: "Please show me something to be thankful for that I've never noticed before; give me an insight, Lord, into what I really possess."

The Lord's intervention is the best possible antecendent during the day.

## Virtue and Rewards

Sometimes, even after we've zeroed in on a positive behavior and co-opted negative antecedents into more benign cues, we still find ourselves spinning our wheels. Somehow getting off dead center is a real chore. The old habit is so well established and has acquired so many cozy allies; the new one gets pushed around at the drop of an impulse. Yes, it's true, action is the key to more action, but how do you break through to that first liberating act?

In cases where new behaviors need an extra push, you can try coming up with a system of rewards, or positive reinforcement. In behavior modification it is adviced that the reward happen only if the desired behavior happens, that it come immediately after the desired behavior, and that it be something with a stronger pull than what you're trying to get rid of.

As soon as we start talking about incentives for doing good we run into problems. After all, isn't virtue supposed to be its own reward? It seems rather unspiritual to seek some goody after every righteous act.

These concerns are legitimate. Virtue must never become simply a means to get something else. At the same time we need an alternative to our traditional means of dealing with habits old and new: negative reinforcement. Christians have developed that to a fine art over the years; we've devised countless ways of punishing ourselves for doing wrong. The discomforts of guilt, instead of driving us to confession, are turned into a whip driving us to perform more. Everything from disapproving glances to fire and brimstone has been misused as a means of extorting right behavior from our poor, weak flesh.

Guilt (and fear of judgment) has only one object: confession. Our right behavior must be motivated by something else: acceptance, a new identity, hidden treasure, the power of the Word. Positive reinforcement can be part of that healthy motivation. It simply works better than negative reinforcement. Remember, *we want to keep our aim more on the good quality we're pursuing than on the sin or habit we're avoiding.*

Rewarding behavior doesn't necessarily turn that behavior into a meaningless duty; changed behavior can sometimes change attitudes. In an experiment conducted by Philip Captain, high school students who were rewarded for reading Scripture each day "showed a significant increase in positive attitudes toward their Bible reading."

## Celebrate the Virtue

Here's the first step toward positive reinforcement: enjoy the virtue itself. A surprising number of us have never learned to do that. We have been trained to focus on the vast distance between our own pathetic efforts and the cosmically high holiness of God. We fall so short of the ideal. That perspective is fine for leading us to seek Jesus as Savior. But after we have been justified by faith, it is no longer appropriate to think primarily in terms of distance. We are now adopted as the Almighty's sons and daughters. Our position in Christ takes us up to heavenly places at God's right hand. From that perspective, the Father does not view our experience as pathetically inadequate. He delights in our first stumbling little steps as much as any father watching his toddler learn to walk.

Religious people nurtured on starkly black-and-white morality are vulnerable to the trap of compulsive perfectionism which sees everything in all-or-nothing terms, what one psychologist labels the "Saint-or-Sinner" syndrome. That one outburst of anger ruins all the malleability you've experienced. That one B in a straight-A record spells complete failure. That one spoonful of ice-cream indulged in means you are *off* the diet, so you might as well eat the whole quart. A constant fear of mistakes can neutralize our best efforts.

Even more of us neutralize effort through humility-by-default. We're always afraid of becoming proud of our spiritual accomplishments and so constantly denigrate our efforts: "Oh yes I may have prayed for obnoxious Susan today, but I have so *far* to go; I still can become so *filled* with resentment." We put ourselves and our successes down in order to remain humble. But in doing so we actually despise God's work of grace. If Jesus could commend the criminal on the cross for turning his face toward the Redeemer in a gesture of faith, then He will certainly appreciate our feeble steps, too. We need to rejoice in the expression of virtue, however modest it may be. Otherwise we'll humble ourselves right into capitulation. If our successes are so pathetic, what's the point of trying?

There's a difference between enjoying victories and becoming conceited over them. As long as you are rejoicing over a partnership with God and focused on hidden treasure, your satisfaction will remain healthy. It's only when you start imagining you've been walking solo, have arrived at the pinnacle, and "own" the virtue, that pride starts putting up its obstacles.

Rejoice in your steps forward. That's the first way you can positively reinforce virtue as a habit. Thank God for your success; savor it. Generally virtue does bring its own tangible rewards. Yes, it does feel better to pray for Susan than to seethe over her peevishness. Yes, it's great to experience a surge of thanks instead of a spell of the blues. My reward for overcoming resentment toward Big Wally the football player was the new relationship I could enjoy with him.

So affirm your behavior as an expression of the virtue you've chosen. Yes, this is one small step toward hidden treasure. Yes, God's way is best. Don't just grimly go on to the next step hoping that someday it all may add up to something worthy of the holy God up there. Your Father is shouting for joy beside you.

## External Reinforcement

Still, habits are habits because they're well dug in. You may need to make the reward of virtue more prominent in order for it to be reinforcing. You may require a more obvious celebration. In that case, try to make the reward fit the success as closely as possible. The "internal reinforcement" we've just discussed can be tied to some form of "external reinforcement." For over-eating: Decide you'll buy a new dress when you lose those twenty pounds. Depression: Take a break from work and listen to some beautiful music when you think of something to be thankful for. Lust: Go out to dinner to celebrate a mutually edifying encounter with someone of the opposite sex.

The same reinforcer, however, if used over and over again, tends to lose its effectiveness. So it may be necessary to come up with a variety of ways to celebrate your virtue-objective.

Finally, as a last resort, you may have to adopt a pattern of reinforcement that is more arbitrary. A habit like swearing in anger may be so unconscious and frequent that you need something more immediate and tangible as positive reinforcement for malleability. Try having your favorite soft drink whenever you thank God for some obstacle instead of blowing up. Enjoy the virtue; enjoy the drink. Just make sure the reward is always dependent on the desired behavior.

When I was about five my father came up with a way to keep me from sucking my thumb at night. I'd been weaned from its comforts during the day, but frequently reverted back to it while sleeping. Instruction in the benefits of quitting was of no value, of course. I was already persuaded; I could see good reason every time my oldest brother smiled — and revealed his braces. So instead of haranguing me, Dad drew up a chart and tacked it to my bedroom door. Each evening, he said, he would put some tape around my thumb. If the tape was dry in the morning I'd get a check mark on the chart. He promised that, after I'd earned thirty marks, he'd buy me a genuine just-what-I-wanted Big Kid's Bicycle.

This sounded like a plan. I went to sleep dreaming of a shiny red bike and woke up with wonderfully dry tape on my thumb. The reward worked its way into my subconscious and began giving the orders. I racked up thirty check marks in a spirit of joyful expectation, and went off to claim the prize.

Positive reinforcement of desired behavior does more for you than all the righteous abuse you can heap on a bad habit. A tangible reward simply makes better company in there where the orders are given. This type of immediate, external incentive is most useful in the short term, to help you get off dead center. As soon as your new habit gets a foothold, start slowly withdrawing the arbitrary reward; reinforce the behavior intermittently. Enjoy the success itself more and more. The point is to progress to where the experience of virtue becomes more rewarding than the old unhealthy habit.

With all these techniques for coming out with a desired behavior, it may seem that goodness becomes quite calculated and therefore loses much of its value. Doesn't real virtue need to be spontaneous to a certain extent, a genuinely felt expression? Yes, but there's usually some "disciplined training in righteousness" behind that expression. If you are put off by techniques and frequencies and antecedents and rewards, just remember that you are laying a temporary groundwork for future skills. The gymnast needs to get certain movements down pat before launching into her individual statement of grace and agility. The ice skater must practice and become fluent in required routines before breaking out in more creative ones. Beginning a good habit may not seem very spontaneous, but it's necessary to get those first few steps going if we are ever to walk with grace.

## *Summary: Behavior*

The last three chapters have focused on strategies which climax in specific behavior change. They create three more expanding circles which work together toward that end.

Chapter 4 talked about adopting a counterpoint virtue.

**Your aim**
*Where you want to go, not what you want to avoid.*

**Hidden treasure**
*Concentrate on visible virtue-objectives, not just the empty space on the other side of sin.*

**Qualities in Jesus**
*Pursue Christ's character made specific: solid sensitivity, malleability, resilient contentment, sharp mercy.*

**The challenge**
*You're acquiring a skill, not facing pass/fail tests.*

As this biblical script is written by the Spirit into our minds, it forms more neural pathways, more self-reinforcing circuits of thought. Our expanding circle of offense pushes that alluring image of the old habit farther out toward the periphery, and creates more and more room for the counterpoint virtue to capture our imagination (see figure 7).

Chapter 5 explained how to make sure we're armed.

**Battle cries**
*Instead of ducking your head, become a witness for the prosecution.*

**Spiritual weapons**
*Wield the entire arsenal: Mighty Warrior, Crucified Son, Powerful Spirit, Angelic Host.*

**Preemptive strikes**
*Don't duel with temptation; overwhelm it with the Word.*

This expanding circle relates to our spiritual stance — how we face the enemy when he makes a sudden appearance. By forming a deeper groove in our minds about the arsenal God has placed in our hands (see figure 8), we push the old timidity and fear responses farther and farther away from us and create more room for a bold wielding of our spiritual weapons.

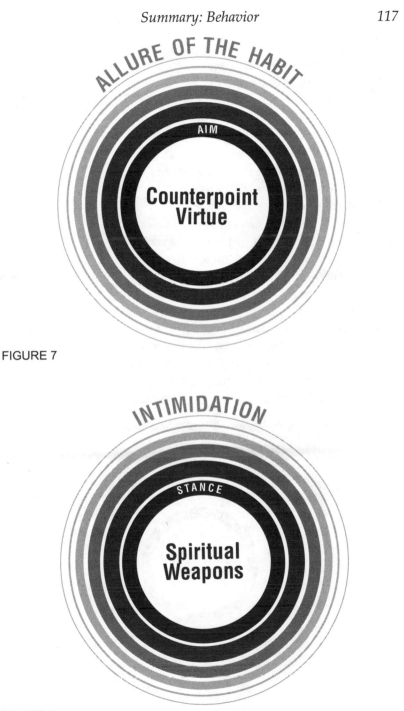

FIGURE 7

FIGURE 8

Chapter 6 detailed the steps we must take to express our counterpoint virtue in action.

**Counterpoint behavior**

> *Select a simultaneous and incompatible action*
> *which excludes the unhealthy habit.*

**Antecedents**

> *Avoid or remove bad behavior cues.*
> *Use unavoidable cues as an early warning system.*
> *Ask God for a rendezvous.*

**Reinforcement**

> *Learn to enjoy successes.*
> *Make the reward fit the new behavior.*
> *Use temporary, arbitrary rewards when necessary.*

This growing circle of action works with the previous two strategies to create a strong neural pathway for our new habit. Keeping our aim on that virtue-objective helps behavior change to remain a positive pursuit and prevents the enemy from taking back territory he has lost. As we reinforce the new behavior pattern, it is imprinted deeply in our brains, expanding to supplant old, habitual responses with more new ones more of the time (see figure 9).

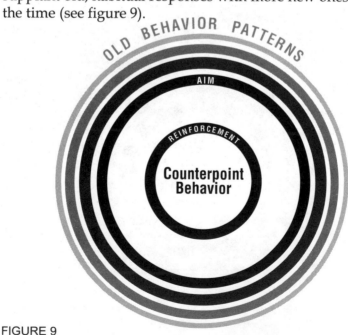

FIGURE 9

# 7

# Moods and Momentum

A FEW years ago, Gifts Unlimited of Scarborough, Ontario, offered to the public "an exciting new watch with mystical properties." Its breathless ad stated: "The watch face changes color from an ominous black through six distinctive stages to a vibrant blue. Many people believe that the colors do reflect inner moods and feelings. Judge for yourself, test the watch's colour against your own emotions." The company even provided a key to interpreting these revelatory hues. Black signified heavy stress, brown tenseness, and yellow anxiety. Blue, however, told good news: you feel fine. Royal blue was even better: you're in top form.

This Mood Watch, which presumably measured body temperature, proved to be a popular timepiece. The people at Gifts Unlimited understood how intrigued we all are by our emotions, and how much we'd like to get a handle on them. The idea of actually being able to measure your moods, however far-fetched, carries an implicit promise of controlling them.

In the last chapter, we went through a step-by-step process of initating changes in our lives. We saw how to rewrite our minds with new thought and behavior patterns. But it's not often easy to stick to a certain strategy. We're not always heading resolutely and earnestly in one direction; we're more here and there. Our moods change. Some of us are veritable chameleons of feeling.

## Just My Mood

Up-and-down emotions tend to be a problem for most of us wrestling with a stubborn habit. They can sabotage the best-laid plans. We make some headway for a few days and establish some successes. But one morning we wake up feeling blah. The day looks wretched. We just can't get up the energy or resolve to continue the struggle, and so decide to chuck it all. It's back to square one again.

Emotions generally win out over rational resolutions; feelings are up close and personal, reasons lecture us at arms length. Emotions are simply more "present" in our minds than abstract goals.

In the past, Christians have been advised to simply ignore their emotions. The spiritual life, we were told, is run on faith, not feelings. That's certainly true, but sometimes it's pretty hard to untangle our faith from our feelings. We may even fear there will be very little belief left once the emotions are cut away.

Feelings as part of the whole spectrum of mental activity which human beings continually engage in. That activity takes on many different emotional hues, from the cold, mechanical action of an accountant adding up his figures, to the warmer but disciplined imagination of a philosopher trying to merge several concepts, to the hot reaction of a lover who's been slapped in the face.

At different times we experience an orderly succession of thoughts, a creative jumble of thoughts, a wild rush of thoughts. Some thoughts remain in a jar on a shelf in our minds. Other thoughts break through and speed up our pulse. Some come and go as efficiently as a UPS package, while others slither around in our heads for days and leave messy traces.

Feelings are simply thoughts which affect us more than other thoughts. We can't just ask them to step outside while we try to deal with this habit. Nor can we dissect them very easily from thinking processes as a whole.

A supply clerk checking in for the graveyard shift at his factory was warned of a small box that had been left on the loading dock. Printed on all sides were the words: "*Danger! Do Not Touch!*" Everyone had been told to stay clear of the parcel until management could analyze the situation. The clerk didn't even want to breathe near the thing and was greatly relieved when a supply foreman arrived in the morning. He donned gloves and safety glasses and slowly, gingerly opened the box. Inside he discovered twenty-five signs which read: "*Danger! Do Not Touch!*"

Sometimes negative emotions become in our minds what that package became on the loading dock. They're bad. We wish they'd go away; we try to step around them. But everything we do is influenced by that nasty box lodged in our brains.

It would help a great deal if we understood those vaguely negative feelings as simply signs that point elsewhere. They are not so terribly toxic in themselves. They are reactions to any number of events or memories or biological processes that pass through our lives. We don't have to know every little unpleasant thing the signs point to. We can just accept the presence of the box and go on to deal with the basic realities that make it necessary.

In this chapter we'll look at resources which relate to emotional stability. We need all the help we can get in this area. Some of us are driven by our moods, the flighty swing of feelings propels us through our daily existence and makes it rather erratic. The Irish poet Thomas Moore knew about such liabilities: "The heart that is soonest awake to the flowers is always the first to be touched by the thorns."

We need a way to make the positive side of our feelings move us forward more consistently. We need rewriting that reaches the level of emotions. That starts not by our focusing on emotions directly, but by aiming at God more directly.

## Patterns of Praise

Praise is a very old habit in the Christian tradition which must be rediscovered from time to time. It's usually encased in once-a-week liturgy amidst solemn and soporific surroundings. But praise belongs even more in the devotional life of the individual; that's where it produces the most spiritual energy and that's where it can have the greatest effect on our emotional life.

Merlin Carothers has documented the power of praise quite dramatically in his testimony *Prison to Praise*. In the book *Answers to Praise* he tells story after story of people finding solutions to a welter of problems — from simple discouragement to infidelity to drug addiction. Carothers believes, and demonstrates, that God's intervening power is unleashed when people adopt a pattern of praise and thanksgiving in their lives. Not everyone will buy praise power as the cure-all for every human difficulty, but it certainly seems a greatly underrated resource in the world.

How do we incorporate this spiritual discipline? First we've got to think about God as a person with certain qualities, not just as a being who gives us things. We find it pretty easy to thank Him for nice days, good grades, and new cars; we can click off our blessings. But praise is about God Himself — looking into the face of the Loved One, not just thinking about what we can get out of Him.

Mark Twain's wife detested her famous husband's habit of swearing and tried many times to reform his tongue. One day the writer cut himself while shaving and blew through his entire store of expletives. When he'd finished, his wife steadily repeated every phrase. Twain turned from the mirror and replied, "You have the words, dear, but you don't know the tune."

Often in our praise, which is the counterpoint of cursing, we recite the words without really getting the tune. Something must jog us into praise; we need the moral equivalent of hammering our thumb. We need eureka: seeing something to truly admire in our Lord. That's the stimulus that will help us praise with something equivalent to the gusto of a sailor spewing epithets.

Praise God for who He is. This is the best way we have of looking directly at the Lord of the Universe. We remember the face that we stare at; we enjoy the qualities of the Loved One which we describe. The affection spoken out loud leaves a deeper impression.

If all this seems a bit esoteric, you've got a lot of help in Scripture; the psalms offer us one hundred and fifty ways to compliment our Heavenly Father. Out of the abundance of material in Scripture which inspires divine admiration, I've collected and paraphrased a few of my favorites:

*God Almighty enthroned in Heaven*
*His encircling radiance is like a rainbow in the clouds;*
*His feet rest on a pavement of lapis lazuli clear as the sky*
*itself;*
*His garments are dazzling white as no launderer on earth*
*can bleach them,*
*fragrant with myrrh, aloes and cassia;*
*His arms and feet glow like burnished bronze refined in a*
*furnace.*

*The Lord God's face shines like the sun in full strength,*
*How blessed are those who walk in the light of His counte-*
*nance;*
*His eyes blaze like flames of fire,*
*the Lord searches all hearts.*
*Rays flash forth from His hand —*
*there is the hiding of His power;*
*His right hand upholds me and my name is inscribed on His*
*palm.*

*Our God is a consuming fire,*
*the voice of the Lord shakes the earth,*
*mountains melt like wax at Your presence;*
*Yet a buised reed You will not break*
*nor a dimly burning wick snuff out.*

*Prince of Peace*
*a Refuge and Fortress to me,*
*You make the dawn and sunset shout for joy*
*and still the tumult of the peoples.*

*The voice of the Lord is like the sound of many waters.*
*Your speech thunders majestically,*
*Your words are pure*
*like silver refined in a crucible*
*seven times purified.*

*Oh Father to the fatherless and Judge for the widows*
*You make a home for the friendless*
*You visit the earth and cause it to overflow*
*The meadows are covered with flocks*
*and valleys with grain.*

*Even the moon has no brightness*
*and the stars are not pure in Your sight;*
*Yet how many O Lord are Your thoughts toward us;*
*This I know, that God is for me.*
*In Your presence is fulness of joy.*

This is just a sample of the wealth of praise in the Bible; dig into it and come up with your own picture of God. Give thoughts about God some time to sink in; put them in sentences you address back to the Lord. Zestful praise, perhaps more than any other spiritual discipline, impacts our emotions positively.

## The Great Constant

Generally, negative emotions arise from our thoughts getting co-opted by too many past irritants, distant worries, or present failures. For some reason we naturally adhere to whatever is adverse around us and mull it over — and over. As the Welsh proverb says, "Bad news goes about in clogs, good news in stockinged feet." But God is bigger than our problems, better than our failures, more promising than our worries. He simply outweighs everything—if we get a close enough view to place Him in perspective.

Our Heavenly Father can be the great constant in our lives, a peaceful, still spot for the here-and-thereness of our feelings. We may have blown it badly, but there He is, as merciful as ever, the Rock of Ages looming over our difficulties. We may be having a bad week, but He has good plans for all eternity. We may feel intimidated by a chronic habit, but the Almighty crushes His adversaries in the dust.

It's been said that what we praise in other people is a sure indication of our own character. But it's even more true that, in the Spirit, praise to God *creates* character.

Praise means making an investment of emotion in the person of God. Too many of us are connected to Him only by those thoughts in a jar on the shelf. We wave at Him in the distance. Our mental activity heats up in all kinds of situations and for all kinds of causes—except the Lord of heaven and earth. We've got to make an investment of ourselves. That doesn't mean trying to manufacture some kind of sentiment about God; our feelings should never become the target of our devotional life. It simply means spending time looking for cause to praise, savoring glimpses of God.

So if some ugly mood threatens to derail our progress, we don't aim at it; we aim at God. We determine to continue the practice of praise no matter what our circumstances. We don't just say a few words of thankfulness whenever a gorgeous day happens to come by. We echo the praise dug up in our devotional study every day. We praise God when the sky looks muddy, when it's snowing in April, when the check still hasn't come, when the neighbors are noisy, when our favorite team chokes in the Super Bowl. We praise God; He's still there, as much a Good Shepherd, Victorious Warrior, Mighty Refuge, and Prince of Peace as ever, the rainbow of glory still shimmering over His head.

## Becoming Something Else

There's another reason why praise is vital in the process of dealing with chronic sin. As we begin to seriously practice and reinforce specific behaviors that replace a certain habit, and as we attempt to check on our progress, we can fall into another problem — getting tangled up in ourselves. We want to make real change happen, but in that process we can get so wrapped up in our performance that we lose sight of the source of our inspiration. That's when change becomes a chore and negative emotions neutralize us.

There's a paradox here. We have to honestly look at ourselves in order to change, yet if we just look at ourselves we will find it very hard to become something else. Praise gets us out of that bind. It keeps God large enough in the picture. Yes, we have to look at specific behavior, but we deal with it in the setting of God's grace. In our steps of growth, in our successes and failures, we retain the comfort and inspiration of His face, close up. We're talking to God, not just at ourselves. We become someone better, a little different, because praise gives us so much more to see.

# *The Big Mo*

We've examined the up-and-down of feelings; now we'll look at emotional inertia — and acceleration. Besides the value of stability there's also a need for emotional momentum, getting on a roll. Some people are impelled forward, driven toward a healthy goal. Others progress only by the most deliberate exertion, walking, as it were, on the balls of their feet. And often both groups are found in the same church fellowship. Both have the same reasons for changing and the same basic tools. Just why do some people have so much more spiritual momentum than others?

This question is particularly important for those of us whose feelings don't swing much, the stable individuals on the opposite end of the emotional spectrum from the moody. We confidently assert that our emotions remain on an even keel, but sometimes that simply means there aren't enough of them up on deck to move us one way or another. Thoughts safely preserved in a jar on the shelf dominate our daily life. We make enough reasonable decisions, but find it hard to be moved beyond our well-established boundaries. Motivation for real change is hard to come by. Is it possible for the dry souls among us to tap into the Big Mo?

## The Power of Revelation

In studying how people change, I've run across one factor that seems to be a common denominator in all kinds of growth: *making discoveries.*

One summer a suicide fad broke out at the Alabama State Training School for young women convicted of delinquency. Initially, one girl slashed her wrists and another drank poison. When they returned from the emergency room alive and well with exciting stories to relate, suicide became the thing to do. The girls began drinking floor wax, perfume, laundry bleach, even toilet bowl cleaners. Razor blades were especially popular; having bandaged wrists became a kind of badge of honor. Fortunately, none of the teenagers quite succeeded in ending their lives.

The death fad, however, didn't end until one young woman became convinced that life was worth living and that people cared. She spoke up in a group meeting and explained why she wouldn't try to kill herself anymore: "Someday I might have a daughter of my own, and when I do I don't want her looking at my wrists and asking, 'Mommy, tell me what are all those scars?' I mean, what could you say to your own daughter?"

That remark, that piece of enlightenment, was widely quoted and helped finally end the hysteria. It was something the girl herself had discovered. The thought had weight, more weight than all the very sound reasons against suicide which staff members had given her. And it struck the other girls as a revelation, too—yes, what would it be like for your daughter to stare at your scarred wrists?

One of the most dramatic examples of the power of discovery comes from the early life of Helen Keller. As a girl growing up in her own world, shut in by blindness and deafness, she had become almost uncontrollable, a wild child of intense passions.

One day while Helen was playing with a new doll, her longsuffering tutor, Anne Sullivan, placed the toy in her lap and signed out "d-o-l-l" in Helen's palm repeatedly. But the mystery of language remained incomprehensible. Earlier Miss Sullivan had tried to make Helen grasp the word "w-a-t-e-r" with little success. As the tutor continued trying to connect this thing in Helen's lap with the signs on her palm, the girl became agitated. She grabbed the doll and slammed it down on the floor. Feeling the broken fragments of the toy by her feet, she felt a keen sense of delight, not a bit of sorrow or regret.

"In the still, dark world in which I lived there was no strong sentiment or tenderness," Helen later wrote. "I felt my teacher sweep the fragments to one side of the hearth, and I had a sense of satisfaction that the cause of my discomfort was removed."

Miss Sullivan took her unruly charge out into the sunshine and down a path to the well-house, fragrant with the honeysuckle covering it. Someone was pumping water just then. Placing Helen's hand under the cool flow, the tutor spelled out the word "water" again on her other palm. The wild child suddenly stood still, concentrating on Miss Sullivan's fingers.

"Suddenly I felt a misty consciousness as of something forgotten—a thrill of returning thought; and somehow the mystery of language was revealed to me. I knew then that 'w-a-t-e-r' meant the wonderful cool something that was flowing over my hand. That living word awakened my soul, gave it light, hope, joy, set it free!"

Now Helen felt eager to learn. As they returned to the house she began touching objects, and each one quivered with life. She had been given a kind of sight. Words were to "make the world blossom for me, 'like Aaron's rod, with flowers.'" But most remarkable was the impact of Helen's discovery on her moral consciousness: "On entering the door I remembered the doll I had broken. I felt my way to the hearth and picked up the pieces. I tried vainly to put them together. Then my eyes filled with tears; for I realized what I had done, and for the first time I felt repentance and sorrow." Helen's soul had indeed been awakened, moved out of the prison of her selfish impulses. That evening she lay in her bed "and for the first time longed for a new day to come."

Making our own discoveries is one of the most powerful means of stimulating change. Think about religious conversions. People are transformed when the Holy Spirit finally gets through, and the good news about Jesus becomes a great relevation.

Frequently believers experience a heady period of growth even after changing churches or denominations. Their newfound vitality often persuades them that at last they've found God's one true church. And it usually doesn't matter what kind of switch it is: Baptist to Methodist, Presbyterian to Pentecostal, or back the other way. People still are revived. Why? Because they are making discoveries. The new church or denomination looks at Christian doctrine from a slightly different perspective; it emphasizes a part of biblical truth that their previous fellowship neglected. As a result, old verities seem new; the good news strikes them again with force. They grow.

### Formulas and Fire

The dynamic of discovery helps explain why various believers through the ages have concluded that they've isolated *the* secret of the Christian life.

John Bunyan was strolling through the fields one day, feeling deeply troubled and frustrated by his sins, when a phrase from Scripture dropped on him with great force: "Thy righteousness is in heaven." He saw Christ at God's right hand

and his righteousness right there with Him. "It was not my good frame of heart that made my righteousness better, nor yet my bad frame that made my righteousness worse; for my righteousness was Jesus Christ Himself, 'the same yesterday, today, and forever.'"

Following this revelation, Bunyan reported: "Now did my chains fall off my legs indeed. I was loosed from my afflictions and irons; my temptations also fled away . . . Christ! there was nothing but Christ that was before my eyes." John Bunyan became a champion of God's justifying grace.

J. Hudson Taylor spent his time earnestly seeking to abide in Christ on a deeper level. One day, when his "agony of soul was at its height" a sentence in a friend's letter "removed the scales from my eyes." It said, "But how to get faith strengthened? Not by striving after faith, but by resting on the Faithful One."

Taylor realized he'd been working hard to rest in Christ. That was impossible. He caught a glimpse of Christ as the Vine and himself as a branch and "what light the blessed Spirit poured into my soul!" A realization of the rest which "full identification with Christ brings" flooded him with joy. He felt a profound sense of release and peace, knowing that God "is able to carry out His will, and His will is mine." After this transforming experience, Hudson Taylor faithfully proclaimed *The Exchanged Life* as the essence of Christian experience.

Richard Halverson attended a Bible conference five months after his conversion where his already serious contemplation of what plan God might have for his life reached an unbearable intensity. He asked permission to leave but was persuaded to stay for a final talk by a former missionary to Korea.

The man's message seemed aimed directly at Halverson. He recalled: "The issue was very clear: Christ wanted my life in full surrender. I literally broke out in a cold sweat as I realized this."

Later, in a cabin prayer meeting, Halverson accepted God's terms: "This experience of utter yieldedness to the Savior and the consequent joy that filled my life was far more cataclysmic than my conversion. . . . As a result of that experience, the Holy Spirit has always been real to me." For Halverson the big answer became *full surrender.*

People who experience such life-changing moments of enlightenment naturally share their "secret" with others. And those most impressed by a certain message naturally try to make that formula function in their lives. But most of us find it doesn't quite work so magically. We try to see our righteousness in heaven or rest completely in Christ or make a full surrender—and nothing big happens.

The more scholarly argue over the merits of each formula. Should we passively rest in Jesus or actively surrender? Do we just concentrate on our position in Christ or must we concentrate on holiness?

What is lacking in all this is the spiritual momentum created by those original discoveries. God zapped Bunyan, Taylor, and Halverson with the particular truth they needed to hear at the time, and that personal revelation started a big fire. They weren't just trying to imitate someone else's formula.

This isn't to say that truth is subjective. We certainly should examine all theories about the Christian life in the light of biblical information. And those that do have scriptural support possess value and applicability in themselves. The point is that the effectiveness of objective truth often depends on our apprehension of it. If it only sits there neatly arranged on the shelf, it won't move us very far.

### That Your Heart Be Enlightened

Spiritual momentum is created by making discoveries through the aid of the Holy Spirit. Personal revelations propel us toward change. Going over the catechism doesn't. Defending our doctrinal turf doesn't. Listening to the same old stories related in the same old way doesn't.

The most dramatic religious conversions generally accompany the most dramatic discoveries. And conversely, we

usually settle into spiritual slow-motion as our personal discoveries lessen. The period of excited learning fades; we lose
momentum. Most of us accept this settling down as inevitable.
Admittedly, the time of bubbly infatuation following conversion does have its limits. We can't always walk on air; we have
to come down emotionally to some extent. But we don't have
to lose all the momentum; we don't have to settle for spiritual
limbo — just maintaining the faith.

Fortunately God has provided a means for our continuing to make discoveries. We see it in Paul's great hope for believers: "I keep asking that the God of our Lord Jesus Christ,
the glorious Father, may give you the Spirit of wisdom and
revelation, so that you may know Him better." The apostle's
prayer is that "the eyes of your heart may be enlightened" so
that believers may apprehend inspiring truths about their hope,
riches, and power in Christ.

Paul keeps asking his Lord about this. This "Spirit of wisdom and revelation" is a priority, a day-to-day need, of which
he's continually conscious. The apostle prays specifically that
hearts may be enlightened, that people will see on a deeper
level. This is not just a review of the facts, an amassing of the
correct data; it's revelation, personal discovery.

Some of us may be a bit intimidated by this talk of heart
enlightenment and revelation. We're not that mystically in-
clined; we don't have visions. The closest we've come to an
ecstatic religious experience is winning the church league soft-
ball championship.

Not to worry. We've all had occasions of exciting discovery when something we didn't know before turned on our
lights for a few minutes. All genuine learning stimulates. It's
not just adding another jar on the shelf — it actually breaks
through and quickens our pulse. Having the eyes of our heart
enlightened doesn't mean that we fall into a rapture, but simply that we make a real discovery. The truth hits home, carrying
some emotional weight.

So before you open your Bible in the morning, stake your
claim to that Spirit of wisdom and revelation. The Spirit wields

the Word as a sword to make God's truth sink deep. That's a major objective in our devotional life. That's why prayer and Bible study go together so well.

## Strike a Telling Blow

The things we've discussed in previous chapters all relate to making discoveries in our quiet times. We look for specific revelations that move us through the process of change. Perusing through Hebrews you find the author praying "that none of you be hardened by the deceitfulness of sin." A light goes on. *Yes, that sin didn't just overwhelm me, it conned me. It lied. And I'm a little more calloused to the truth now.* That bit of insight moves you to a more meaningful confession and repentance. You don't want to be hardened; you want to be more responsive to God.

Prayerfully reading in the psalms you find a verse that grabs at your sinking resolve: "I incline my heart to perform thy statutes forever, to the end." The psalmist's faithful-unto-death intensity strikes a chord: *If he could be that committed to the law of Jehovah, surely I can take a firm stand with the crucified Christ.* You begin using this verse as another supporting piece in your statement of will.

Studying 1 Corinthians you run across Paul's statement: "The Lord is for the body and the body is for the Lord." You'd never realized that before. The Lord *for* the body. Him being for our soul or spirit is understandable. But here God Almighty declares that He acts in the best interests of our physical selves. That's why we can use our bodies *for* the Lord, for His glory. This gives you a new way of looking at yourself, another piece to your identity in Christ. And you are encouraged to act as one whose body, as well as soul, has been divinely chosen.

Meditating on Hebrews you find a verse that strikes a telling blow at your problem with anger: "Discipline no doubt is never pleasant, at the time it seems painful, but in the end it yields for those who have been trained by it the peaceful harvest of an honest life." Yes, this is exactly the malleability you're after: a willingness to be disciplined by God, to take the blows as training instead of as incitement to blow up. The verse helps sharpen your aim at the counterpoint virtue. *Yes, I want the peaceful harvest of an honest life, not the painful results of an erratic existence pushed and pulled by a bad temper.* The hidden treasure sparkles a bit more brightly.

You're reading about Christ's temptation in the wilderness where Satan slithers in with a suggestion that his worthy Adversary turn stones into bread and feed Himself. Christ replies, "Man does not live on bread alone, but on every word that comes from the mouth of God." Suddenly you see this familiar verse in a different light, as a great weapon against lust. The flesh has been pressing those hard-core images against you insistently. You've got to have it, turn these stones into bread. Porn is the mechanical, reductionist counterpart to the real sexuality, the real bread, that nourishes us. Sex without commitment is an attempt to turn stones into bread. It's not right — even if you can consume it.

Jesus' response must be mine. *Man doesn't live by bread alone. If a legitimate way of having bread, having intimacy, is not possible right now, I won't resort to stones, to porn. Sex isn't necessary for life; I can live by the words that God speaks to me. They're enough right now.* These verses in Matthew become a revelation that enables you to bear witness against sin: *No, that's asking me to turn stones into bread.* The insight rouses you to battle.

Bad habits don't voluntarily make way for their betters. Don't expect one insight to topple your nemesis — although that has been known to happen. What we're doing here is providing the momentum that will help us keep "doing the law," modifying behavior, as outlined in the previous chapter. Our discoveries will place continual pressure on the old habits and open more and more ground for the new. Through this consistent rewriting of our minds, emotion will slowly become a more reliable ally in our pursuit of hidden treasure.

# 8

# Wielding Our Beliefs

THE ragged, scrawny European expatriates standing in rows in the center of Shantung Compound feared the worst as the Japanese chief of police prepared to read his verdict. They had heard rumors of atrocities in other prisoner-of-war camps in China, and this was the first opportunity for their captors to demonstrate formal retribution.

The "criminal" standing beside the Japanese officer was a small, bespectacled Catholic named Father Darby. He had been caught slipping eggs under his cassock as he prayed by the wall and was discovered to be a key link between sympathetic Chinese villagers outside and the starving inmates.

The chief began his speech in a loud voice, declaring that he was determined to stamp out the black market and would have to make an example of Father Darby, even though it pained him to "punish a man of the cloth." The weary listeners shuddered; would this gentle father be tortured or only shot? The chief announced: "I sentence you to one and a half months of solitary confinement!"

There was a moment's pause, and then the detainees erupted in a jubilant roar that shocked the solemn Japanese official. Father Darby, they knew, had served as a Trappist monk, thriving in the silence and solitude of the same monastery for twenty-five years. And so, as Japanese soldiers shook their heads in wonder, the father marched off to his tiny cell—joyously singing praises.

Solitary confinement would have been a terrible ordeal for most of the people languishing in Shantung Compound. But Father Darby took it as a spiritual opportunity. The only difference between hellish isolation and heavenly peace was his attitude, the way he had come to regard such an experience. William James wrote, "The greatest discovery of my generation is that a human being can alter his life by altering his attitude." Life doesn't come to us directly; it's mediated through our point of view, our mind-set, our assumptions.

According to Albert Ellis and others advocating "cognitive therapies," what an individual says to himself governs the way he feels and acts. In other words, it's not the situation that determines our emotional and behavior responses, but our "self-verbalizations" about the situation we're in. In his work, Dr. Ellis seeks to determine what is irrational in a client's belief system, point out the absurdity of certain assumptions, and help the person adopt a more rational perspective on life. Ellis's "Rational-Emotive Therapy" keys on certain basic self-defeating beliefs, such as: *I should be loved and respected by everyone. I should be competent in everything I do. I am powerless to determine whether I'll be happy or miserable.* These assumptions, when held rigidly, prevent people from adapting to events in a healthy way.

## All Unbeknown to Meself

Beliefs affect our behavior, especially beliefs that have nestled down in our minds as hidden assumptions. They may be harder to get a handle on, but they influence us nonetheless, sometimes sabotaging our well-laid plans for change. Attitudes that have "dug in" often lie behind those vaguely negative feelings that pull us down. We dealt with emotions first because they tend to move us most directly to healthy or unhealthy behavior. And it is not always necessary to untangle all the assumptions that result in certain moods or feelings. Often they will be replaced simply by the weight of other beliefs: our acceptance of forgiveness, identification with Christ or aim at a certain virtue.

But some assumptions hang tough. The carnal nature does not easily let go of reliable allies. There are ideas lurking in the back of our minds which would fade away in embarassment if brought out in the light, but which thrive when kept in semi-secrecy. Sometimes we must throw a spotlight on the beliefs burrowed under our behavior, drag them out by the scruf of their neck, and tell them off. Unless we consciously deal with such attitudes, they will continue to affect us adversely — even if we don't give them conscious assent.

The lie we'd rather not look at can be our worst enemy. An Irishman who'd pledged to a priest that he would abstain from alcohol became terribly thirsty, slipped into a tavern, and ordered lemonade. As the bartender was preparing the drink, he whispered, "And couldn't ye put a little brandy in it all unbeknown to meself?" Sometimes we don't want to take responsibility for those self-serving ideas that have slipped into our subconscious all unbeknown to ourselves.

Rewriting on the level of ideas is required here. We must deal with habits of mind, the filters through which experience comes to us. It's good that we've already begun to tackle behavior because beliefs are more readily jarred to the surface when we're in the process of altering our actions.

Psychology professor Rodger K. Bufford decided one day to confront a chronic problem in his life: quarrels with his wife. In doing so he met up with an assumption: "It had been my standard operating principle that these disagreements were primarily her fault." When he came across passages of Scripture that played rough with his comfortable beliefs, Bufford decided to internalize them. He memorized two verses in Proverbs (12:1 and 26:2) about reaction to criticism which hit a bull's eye. Those phrases, "He who hates reproof is stupid" and "A curse without cause does not alight," sank deep. He acknowledged their truth and determined to reflect more when critized instead of just becoming upset. Subsequently he reported, with professorial understatement: "When the next dispute with my wife developed, I was promptly reminded of these principles and prompted to react in a somewhat different manner than that which had been my custom. The results were gratifying."

It's time to do a bit of brain scanning. Haul out the beliefs that have hunkered down as if elected for life, those incumbents with all the connections, and take a hard look. Think about what you really want to affirm, as opposed to what you've believed by default.

## God Opens His Hand

First let's deal with general assumptions which relate to all kinds of habits and sins. One implicit belief loitering within almost every person contemplating transgression is this: *God is holding something back from me.* Everyone from Eve in the Garden eyeing that lovely fruit on the forbidden tree to Joe Blow in North Hollywood lingering by the entrance to "Exotic Dancers" has bought into that assumption. Deliberate acts of sin presume that God is holding out.

If we were to take this belief out and stand it up in the light, we'd quickly disown it. Why of course the God of heaven and earth is not denying anything good to us. He loves His children. But as a hidden assumption, this ridiculous attitude can go on tripping us up indefinitely. We feel it back there in the dark, urging us to indulge in the forbidden delight: "It's too much fun for God to handle; He's holding out on you." We give our assent in the pressure of the moment, buy into the hoax, and sin. Then the lie burrows back deep into our minds, out of sight, waiting for its next opportunity to nudge us off the track.

So we've got to make this belief come out into the spot-light. We have to consciously face it down: *You've been telling me that God is holding back on me and that's a lie. I don't believe it for a moment.* Then we must crush this assumption with truth from God's Word; we must hold on to the teaching, as Jesus advised, so that the truth can set us free.

Next time you feel that shove in the dark from the old lie, lay it out cold with this verse from Romans: "He who did not spare his own Son, but gave Him up for us all—how will he not also, along with him, graciously give us all things?" Can we really imagine, even half-consciously, that the God who gave up His own beloved Son to be consumed by our accumulated cruelty is going to be chintzy about other blessings? Impossible. He already emptied heaven. He already emptied His own heart. The best has been poured out on our unworthy, indifferent heads. No, God is not holding back. There's no transgression that can offer something better than what God has to give.

The psalmist held up a springtime portrait of nature as an echo of Jehovah's habitual generosity:
"You care for the land and water it;
  you enrich it abundantly . . .
you soften it with showers
  and bless its crops . . .
The meadows are covered with flocks
  and the valleys are mantled with grain;
  they shout for joy and sing."

Every color and form and texture in the rich variety of living things bears witness to a God who blesses. Psalm 85 sums it up in terms of personal experience:
"Better is one day in your courts
  than a thousand elsewhere. . . .
For the Lord God is a sun and shield;
  the Lord bestows favor and honor;
no good thing does he withhold
  from those whose walk is blameless."

With scriptural support like that, you can deal decisively with temptation dropping those old lines and making those cheap moves. Get to the root of its appeal: *You're assuming that God is holding something back from me. That's a lie. My God opens His hand and satisfies the desire of every living thing. He fructifies the earth; He withholds nothing good; He didn't even spare His Son.*

Acknowledge clearly what you do believe. Your beliefs had better stand at attention and be counted, otherwise they'll be silently replaced. Truth affirmed affects behavior. God's truth affirmed sets you free.

## Two Paths

Let's look at another assumption that relates to bad habits in general. Frequently when tempted we will tell ourselves, very quietly, that this is just a little misstep, no big deal. We try to focus on the act itself and cut it off from its results, its meaning. We just want to take this quick detour and bounce right back on the straight and narrow. We want a little break from righteousness.

But of course that's the same old excuse our habits always make, just this once — week after week, year after year. As Samuel Johnson wrote, "The chains of habit are generally too small to be felt until they are too strong to be broken." Again, if that implicit belief really came out in the open, we'd quickly disavow any knowledge of its activities. Sin always matters in God's sight. C.S. Lewis wrote in *The Screwtape Letters*: "The safest road to hell is the gradual one — the gentle slope, soft underfoot, without sudden turnings, without milestones, without signposts."

So we confront the lie head-on, preferrably ahead of time. We grab this assumption that it doesn't matter so much and drag it out of the closet. The truth we must challenge it with is this: *Two paths diverge at my feet; I have to make a choice about who to serve.* Our action directs us down one of two roads: "The path of the righteous is like the first gleam of dawn, shining ever brighter till the full light of day. But the way of the wicked is like deep darkness, they do not know what makes them stumble." We must make our choice very clear, no fudging over a few missteps. We're either following the ever-brighter way of righteousness or we're stumbling down toward deepest night.

Many scripture passages attempt to radicalize our thinking by making us look beyond this present temptation. What does it lead to? What is the end result? God is not going to cancel our ticket to heaven every time we take a sinful detour, but He does want us to concentrate on what our action says, what direction it points toward. Here's Joshua reflecting that theme as he made his greatest speech to the Hebrews, urging them to renew their covenant to Jehovah at Shechem. He said, "But if serving the Lord seems undesirable to you, then choose for yourselves this day whom you will serve, whether the gods your forefathers served beyond the River, or the gods of the Amorites, in whose land you are living. But as for me and my household, we will serve the Lord."

Joshua was saying, "If you're not willing to follow God completely, then face the alternatives; you're either going to be serving the moon-god Nanna, or Egypt's golden calf, or Apis the sacred bull, or bloodthirsty Baal and Ashtoreh who demand the sacrifice of children. Look at the choice you're making."

That's what Scripture pushes us toward. No fuzzy thinking about a little time off from the straight-and-narrow. Look at the alternatives: you're going to be serving the devil or serving the Lord. Make your choice.

So in response we can tell the lie: *You want me to indulge a bit here? Really? You want me to serve the evil one who'd like to put an iron yoke about my neck and confine me in a depraved mind, the one who longs for the day when he can shut me out in his darkness, weeping and gnashing my teeth?*

Drag out the assumption and blast it with hard light from the Word. As you do this more and more consistently, the old thought patterns that greased your way into sin will reshape into new radicalized thought patterns that look down the road and fasten on that vision of a life growing brighter and brighter until the "full light of day."

# Specialized Assumptions

## Yelling As Passion

Now that we've looked at some general assumptions, let's tackle beliefs that lie behind specific behaviors. Take the habit of yelling at people, yelling at your kids, your spouse, other drivers.

I've felt around in the dark and discovered an assumption which seems to reinforce that kind of abusive anger in me as a male of the species. The belief is this: *Shouting makes me more of a man.*

Think about revenge fantasies. Someone has wronged us or we hear about some outrageous injustice, and we vent our anger by imagining a confrontation with the wretched perpetrator in which we beat him to a pulp — and then walk off amidst admiring female glances.

Shouting is part of that macho picture. It's verbal violence, knocking down wrongdoers with our words. And often our conscious acknowledgment (after it's too late) that words can seriously wound can't overcome a more deeply imbedded belief: *I shout because I am a man.*

Many women, interestingly enough, seem to harbor a mirror-image assumption: *I yell because I am a woman.* That self-statement is nurtured by the view that females have a right to be "emotional," and to use displays of feeling as a defense against threats. For decades, movies have idealized the fiery woman who throws things at the male lead and ends up riding off into the sunset with him. Her tantrums supposedly reveal a deeply passionate nature. No movie, of course, ever shows her throwing things at him or the kids after marriage. That would spoil the myth.

Both women and men need to drag these assumptions out of the closet and turn on the spotlight. Here's a shaft from the book of Colossians: "Put on then as God's chosen ones, holy and beloved . . . patience — which is tireless longsuffering and has the power to endure whatever comes with good temper."

This is the power that counts; this is how we reach our potential — through Christ's Spirit fashioning a good temper out of the jumble of carnal impulses. Men wanting to be regarded as strong and women wanting to be regarded as deeply passionate need to acknowledge that yelling, losing our temper, negates both. Inner strength requires self-control. Strong attachments require patient, tireless desire.

Contrary to popular assumption, it is the shouter, the abuser, who displays his weakness: "Like a city whose walls are broken down is the man who lacks self-control." Show me a man who habitually shouts at people and I'll show you an individual whose manhood is gutted.

So the next time you fantasize about blasting someone as Mr. Big, remember those broken-down walls. Don't let the lie sell you short. The next time you start yelling because, as a female, you must be all but helpless before your emotions, remember what real passion is all about. Make those false assumptions come out and take the heat. Consciously focus on what you *do* believe before God: *My calling is to reflect His power through self-control, through being malleable.*

After your first affirmation of such a truth you may still find yourself slipping back into the old assumption. Just keep repeating your positive belief, keep reinforcing the new perspective. It will soon overpower the lie.

### Sex with X

Most of us will be tempted at one time or another by a member of the opposite sex and be required to make a stand on the line between admiration and adulterous fantasy. In our struggle against the lust that wages war against our souls, it helps to look carefully at what we believe. We may uncover this assumption hanging about in the dark: *Sex with X is more exciting than sex with my spouse.* That other attractive person, that mysterious X, becomes the greener grass on the other side of the fence. This belief lies at the root of a whole spectrum of sexual sin.

But here we may feel we're up against a wall. It may very well be that X *is* more physically attractive. There are plenty of gorgeous people out there. How do we deal with that? Are we supposed to make ourselves believe that X is ugly, simply assume by faith that he or she is a sexual dud?

No. Evaluating X sexually is something we need to avoid in the first place. Instead we focus on a different, positive belief, acknowledging the fact that 90 percent of sexual fulfillment involves the *quality of our relationship*, not the quality of the plumbing or the perfection of the fixtures. Physical attributes can certainly be stimulating, but they of themselves don't sustain sexual intimacy. It's the relationship, the commitment, that provides an environment where sexuality can blossom.

I've seen the husbands of bounteous women lose interest in them completely. We all see perfectly stunning Hollywood couples break up with the regularity of clockwork. People fall for someone new, whatever they have at home, if their relationship has weakened.

Having good sex depends more than anything else on having good communication with our spouse. Yes, some babe or hunk walking down the street may seem exciting; but that's not where genuine sexual fullfilment lies. It's not better out there; super mechanical sex just doesn't go very far.

So in our dodging of the seductive around us, we need to make sure our beliefs are on line. Are we assuming that sex with X is the ultimate thrill and that we must settle for something proper but not very exciting with our spouse? X doesn't have the answers. A better relationship with our husband or wife is the answer.

Here's some light from Proverbs to throw on the subject:
"May your fountain be blessed,
    and may you rejoice in the wife of your youth.
A loving doe, a graceful deer —
    may her breasts satisfy you always,
    may you ever be captivated by her love."

The godly ancients knew where it was at. If you're going to have sexual fulfillment, it's going to be found at home. This applies to both men and women, of course. That "loving doe" is largely in the mind of the beholder; it's up to you to be captivated by her or his love.

The whole of Proverbs 5 sheds some very pointed light on the deceptions that accompany those going out to seek extramarital pleasures. The writer warns of lips dripping honey that turn into bitter gall. Proverbs 7 reinforces the points, picturing the seduced as oxen sent meekly off to slaughter and assuring us that the perfumed bed of the adulterer is a highway to the grave.

We've got to drag the lies out of hiding. Don't give them any spot of refuge. Affirm what you do believe. Say it out loud if necessary. Say it to your spouse by all means: *You are my loving doe, I wish always to be captivated by your love.*

## My Expectations

How about resentment, stewing over the person who has wronged us or who just rubs us the wrong way? What kind of thinking leads into this habit? Resentment can appear to be pure emotion, pure gut reaction. But there's usually something cognitive, something we believe, loitering in the background.

Try this assumption on for size: *Other people should meet my expectations.* At first this idea doesn't appear very harmful or even very unreasonable, but it's an exceedingly dangerous premise to have hanging around. The danger lies in the "should" part of this belief. It's one thing to *hope* that people will meet our expectations or be happy when people meet our expectations; it's quite another to believe that they *should* do so.

Living out of our naturally self-centered mind-set as we do, it's very easy for us to extend our desires into rights and demands. Nothing seems more sensible than that our will be extended out into the world, and when we find that it's other people who most often get in the way of our will—well, they just shouldn't be that way.

Of course sometimes other people do wrong us; we are sinned against. Countering resentment doesn't mean that we simply lie down after every blow and let circumstances plow over us. It's appropriate for us to labor for what we believe is right—even in the face of opposition. On occasion we have to work at cross-purposes with other people or confront those who make mistakes. However, what we *don't* have to do is work under the burden of indignation over their failure to meet our expectations. That's when resentment slides in and turns positive energy into negative anger.

It's those thwarted expectations that keep us going in circles. *Why oh why did she do that? She had no right. How could he possibly be so insensitive?* We just won't let go of that inarticulated demand that other people behave in a certain way. We rehearse the wrong over and over in our minds, building a consuming fire with all the friction of this terrible act rubbing against us.

So when feeling offended, we must first deal with our unrealistic expectations. And here's why they are unrealistic: "All have sinned and fallen short of the glory of God." Familiar belief, yes, but one which we need to consciously acknowledge. Other people are *not* going to meet all our expectations. People forget important dates, neglect loved ones, suspect strangers, interject the wrong words, blow the right opportunity. People fail. Acknowledging human sinfulness also means facing our own. We don't have an omniscient perspective; we don't see every situation in the right light; we judge people for the wrong reasons and misinterpret verbal and nonverbal signals.

When God is disappointed that "we all like sheep have gone astray," He reacts as a Good Shepherd. When God's closest friends let Him down in Gethsemane, He shows sympathy: "The Spirit is willing, but the body is weak." Looking at ourselves and others through the light of God's remarks about our sinfulness helps us accept failure. We sorrow over it, and we don't by any means condone it—but we can get through it.

So when you catch a grudge building up inside, drag up that old lie and face it down: *No I do not believe that other people are always going to meet my expectations. I believe we are all weak and sinful, saved by grace.*

**My Plans**

What about depression? Do the blues carry any hidden baggage along with them, or is this emotion just a simple response to a bad day? We're all going to react negatively to gloomy clouds or rebellious children or getting fired. Sadness is a natural and healthy response to adversity. But when sadness persists and spreads into an enveloping malaise, we've got problems. Depression can be defined as a sadness that grows stubborn, taking on a life of its own.

Here's an assumption that commonly gives aid and comfort to the recurring blues: *Life must go according to my plans.* This belief is the twin of the attitude behind a lot of resentment. The difference between depression and resentment is often simply a matter of the latter focusing on one particular culprit, and the former casting a wide-angled glazed look at life in general. Both trip us up over expectations. The pivot that keeps us going round and round in our depression is this little assumption: "should." *I should be happy. My life should have taken a better turn somewhere. That relationship shouldn't have ended.*

Brooding over our losses, we let self-pity seep in and set up housekeeping. It droops over all the furniture, and pretty soon locks us into wall-to-wall depression. Self-pitying thoughts have a tendency to expand exponentially. Dwelling on some unfortunate incident quickly brings on a host of similar losses as supporting cast.

We need to bring the healthy response of sadness to a close before it settles down into self-pity and prostrates our emotional life. Taking on our hidden assumption will help. After you've acknowledged your loss emotionally (and of course different losses recquire greatly varying periods of mourning), declare what you believe: *I live in a world dominated by sin. Life doesn't always go according to my plans. But this misfortune is not a total disaster; I have God's Word on that: "We know that in all things God works for the good of those who love Him."*

The sovereign Lord once gave a wonderful assurance to Judean exiles whose world had fallen apart: "For I know the plans I have for you . . . plans to prosper you and not to harm you, plans to give you hope and a future." God could work for good even in the ashes of Jerusalem.

## Errors Exposed

Some of us have acquired the habit of coming unglued whenever our mistakes are pointed out. We just can't handle criticism. It sets off an immediate and enthusiastic counterattack. The assumption lying behind this fortress mentality goes something like this: *Errors exposed threaten my value as a human being.*

People fall into a pattern of defensiveness because they see a much greater danger in mistakes than others do. Their sense of self seems small, and blunders loom very large. But this is a pattern of thinking that can be rewritten.

The next time you feel like blasting back with both barrels when someone suggests you part your hair on the other side, stop and stare down that assumption that's egging you on. *My fallibility does not threaten my identity in God's eyes. I've been purchased by the Blood of Christ, accepted in the Beloved in spite of my mistakes. I can afford to acknowledge imperfections before other people.*

You have to let go of that false belief, even though it has been playing over and over in your mind. It's a lie; it doesn't square with what you really believe about your position before the Lord, about your identity both as a sinner and as a chosen child of God.

Affirming what we believe does help set us free from chronic sins. Some habits are more deeply rooted in attitudes than others; some of our discoveries about the assumptions undergirding unhealthy behavior will be more liberating than others. But in every case, clarifying our beliefs based on God's Word has value; it's one more weapon in our spiritual arsenal, one more way we are sanctified "by the truth."

# 9

# A Partner in the Pursuit

In the 1920s a series of experiments were conducted at Western Electric's Hawthorne, Illinois, plant to determine how changes in the working environment might affect productivity. Women assembling telephone relays were evaluated while working under twenty-four different conditions. The amount of light, the number and length of rest breaks, and the length of the workday were the principle variables. What the engineering psychologists discovered was that production kept increasing—no matter what factors were changed. This came to be known as the Hawthorne Effect, "any increase in performance that is the by-product of attention." What this means is that workers will turn out more widgets no matter what you change—paint the walls green, paint them yellow, give everyone uniforms, take them away—it's all the same. The key difference is that someone is paying attention.

More recently those evaluating the original Hawthorne experiments have concluded that "information feedback and differential rewards" were also involved. But the mystique of the Hawthorne effect persists, and still explains a lot of things that happen in daily life. We do better when people are paying attention to what we're doing. Our actions seems to matter more. And if the observer is someone we care about, our motivation becomes that much stronger.

## Souls in Progress

Scott Sweet understood. This gangly, bespeckled fellow missionary who laughed from deep in his throat and studied the Word with great care could smile empathetically when I talked about my struggles with lust or mentioned the threat of some soft-porn display in a neighborhood store. And I knew exactly what he meant when he described that pull of the flesh which can turn all our brave stands to dust. But most importantly Scott resonated with that passion to be pure which those who've struggled long against a cleaving habit sense most urgently.

In our moments of fellowship there was an excitement between us. We weren't just discussing theory; we were talking right now: *This is where I'm at.* I still vividly recall his New England voice, his wild gestures and sympathetic eyes as we shared war stories on the stairs between our apartments. I still can hear the album we listened to: "Saved," Bob Dylan's experiment in fundamentalist folk rock. We both reverberated with that raucous, dead-earnest call to persevere: "You're gonna serve the Devil or serve the Lord." I remember everything because our spiritual lives turned real then, our souls-in-progress passed back and forth as spontaneously and accessibly as Polaroid snapshots. This sharing proved synergistic; we pushed each other to nobler effort, without pointedly trying. In talking about our very common struggle we produced momentum, a third force more than the sum of our two parts.

## Magnifying Our Resources

In Scott Sweet, I discovered one of the greatest weapons a person can wield *for* holy behavior and *against* sinful habit—

a partner in the pursuit. Every resource of the Spirit which we employ is magnified when we talk with a friend about it. We don't realize that because fellowship so often pales into a weekly formality. We drive to church, do the hymns and prayer, sit for half an hour listening to an edifying monologue, shake a few hands, and go home. This predominantly passive, anonymous worship is a far cry from New Testament communion. The power of fellowship is in the Spirit shared, in life shared. Here's how real fellowship helps us say goodby to the same old sin and welcome in a new virtue.

## Encouragement

The writer of Hebrews gives us this classical exhortation regarding fellowship: "And let us consider how we may spur one another on toward love and good deeds. Let us not give up meeting together . . . but let us encourage one another. . . ." What kind of "meeting together" can this refer to? Surely not just a seat on the same pew. It implies stimulating exchanges related to what's happening right now. General talk as a group about abstract principles is a very inefficient way of stirring up others to active goodness. The most potent interaction is always specific, personal, and face-to-face.

While working at a Christian language school in Japan, I got tired of greeting the other teachers with the same old banalities every day. As we passed in the hallway, retrieved our lessons from the lounge, or chatted in between classes, our conversation was pleasant enough, but usually without content. It seemed ironic. Here we were in this utterly secular society trying to present the gospel through our Bible classes and evangelistic meetings, trying hard to help our Japanese friends see the light — and yet that light never seemed to flicker between us. If the gospel was indeed, as we presented it, the great Answer for humanity, why did it raise so few echoes in our daily life?

So I got together with a few buddies and we decided to replace our "Hey-Howya-doin' — Ok-Nice-day" routine with one simple question, "What did you learn today?" Many of us were trying to develop a consistent time of devotions, spurred on as we were by the task of making Christianity real to people who drew a blank when the word "God" was mentioned. What if we tried to share something specific we'd discovered through our time in prayer and the Word?

Soon everyone was joining in. The fact that we were asking each other about *right now* helped a lot of us dig more purposely in the Word for something definite to share. And talking about some useful principle reinforced that truth in our minds. We were all helping each other grow. That ethereal pious word "fellowship" took on flesh and blood. The teachers' lounge and hallway of our English school were never quite the same again.

We were fortunate to have several sharing partners there at the school. But all you need is one, someone who knows about your particular pursuit and can ask you the question, "How did you do today?"

Get a regular time to meet, say once a week. Have a clear goal in mind. Covenant together to pursue a certain quality, acquire a certain skill. Don't let your fellowship water down into vague platitudes. Like two alcoholics in AA clinging together for dear life, you promise to stand by each other and stay in the struggle til sober.

Honesty is terribly important. You've got to get down to the nuts-and-bolts of change. But don't let frankness turn into lament. Moaning over the long arm of the habit or your lengthy record of failure shouldn't dominate the sharing time. Just as in your individual fight, so in your fight together, major in what you're aiming at, talk up that virtue-objective.

In his first letter to the Thessalonians, Paul points to the primary fact undergirding all our acts of encouragement: "He died for us so that, whether we are awake or asleep, we may live together with him. Therefore encourage one another and build each other up." God has given up His life in order to bring us into union with Himself. We all share a common destiny as people rescued by the cross. We're on the same road together; we're going to live together with Christ forever. The more we communicate with each other about the steps we're taking on that road, the more real and magnetic our ultimate goal becomes.

## Accountability

Acquiring a partner in our pursuit also helps us become accountable for our actions to someone else. Keeping things private makes it easier to lie to ourselves, to ignore little slip-ups, to fudge about changes. The recalcitrant self has a thousand ways of wiggling out of conviction and into comfort. But if we put all the cards on the table in front of a friend, the old man of sin has much less room to work in.

Two Zen monks were travelling together down a muddy road during a downpour. Rounding a bend they met a lovely girl in a silk kimono who couldn't get across the intersection. One monk spread his arms and offered to help with a friendly, "Come on, girl." She smiled gratefully and was carried across the road, unsullied.

The second monk did not speak until they reached a temple that night. Finally he could no longer restrain himself: "We monks don't go near females," he said in a troubled voice, "especially young, pretty ones. Why did you do that?"

The other looked up and said, "I left the girl back there on the road. Are you still carrying her?"

Partners in the pursuit can often illuminate what we miss in our instinctive defense of the self. They shed light on our blind spots and help us become more transparent. Paul understood how easily we can be fooled and calloused by sin, and he presented personal, regular encouragement as the antidote: "But encourage one another daily, as long as it is called today, so that none of you may be hardened by sin's deceitfulness."

Establish accountability from the start. Promise each other, while still energized and inspired by a new quest, that you'll always ask and always give straight answers. Knowing that you're going to have to tell your partner about how you're doing motivates you that much more to pursue the virtue instead of the vice. But don't be afraid to admit failure. You're developing a skill, not facing pass/fail tests.

If you reach a point where the struggle becomes perilously intense, call each other—every day if necessary. Claim the power of united prayer. There's nothing like togetherness in moral combat to bind two people into the kind of fellowship that is treasured for a lifetime.

### Consistency

Finally, a sharing partner will bring stability and continuity into our pursuit of the good life. We all have our individual up and down days, and that pattern is rarely in perfect synch with someone else's. So our partner is likely to be up, or at least even, when we're down. Their supportive presence helps smooth out the rough times that can derail us so much more quickly when we're alone. Sometimes they keep grace alive for us. As the Pioneer Girls adage says: "A friend hears the song in my heart and sings it to me when my memory fails."

Committed partners-in-the-pursuit often can function as a miniature body of Christ. God promises to come close wherever two or more are gathered in His name. So you be strong when the other one is weak, steady when they're shaky. You be an eye when they are only feet. They'll be hands for you when you feel limp and a cool head when you are all hot heart.

Alcoholics Anonymous began the day William Wilson called up a stranger, Dr. Robert Smith, from his hotel in Akron, Ohio. Traveling on a business trip, Wilson had felt a strong urge to drink. Though a dramatic encounter with God had given him the upper hand in his long battle with the bottle, he was still tempted on occasion. So he thumbed through the phone book, called up a church, and asked the minister if he knew of any hopeless drunk he could talk to. The perplexed clergyman referred him to Dr. Smith, a desperate alcoholic who'd been unable to stop drinking.

The two men talked for hours. Neither preached to the other. Mr. Wilson simply told his story quietly, and the urge to take that one drink passed. He'd acquired a partner in his lonely struggle whose sympathetic presence saw him through his moment of great peril.

That's how AA was born. A movement in which equally vulnerable people keep each other afloat—with amazing success. Out of their collective, sinking wills, and a decision to rely on God or a Higher Power, stability and resilience are somehow created. A man will tell of sitting for hours in an all-night cafe, filling a notebook with the sentence: "God, help me make it through the next five minutes." He calls up an AA member at 4:00 A.M. and soon finds strength in the understanding face of a stranger.

That's what fellowship was meant to be. Just the presence of another believing, struggling person is often enough to nudge us out of our rut or dispell our doldrums. There they are in the flesh, a part of Christ, standing with us. Praise God for brothers and sisters. We need to acknowledge and affirm the shining example we see in others. During their brightest moments, they model for us the graces that we long to experience.

## Why We're Reticent

Although the benefits of having a partner in the pursuit are significant, a lot of us still hesitate to form such alliances, even with fellow Christians. We have our reasons. First, we're probably embarassed-to-tears about that private sin. Talking to someone about it is the last thing on our minds. *I'll work on it myself, thank you.*

But this area of present spiritual struggle is precisely where fellowship becomes real. All the nice talk about sisterhood and brotherhood is a lot of schlock if we can't open up about our needs, tell someone where we're at. Paul reminded the Corinthians that he'd spoken freely to them and opened wide his heart. He urged them, "As a fair exchange . . . open wide your hearts also."

We don't have to spill out our latest transgressions every week in church. But it would help enormously if we could bare our souls with at least one other trusted friend in Christ.

Then there are the male problems. For some reason, whether it's genes or too many John Wayne movies or just laziness, we men have a real problem opening up with each other. Women seem to get personal effortlessly, but we have to work at it. Well, let's work at it. It's time to get out of the strong-and-silent and defeated rut. We need all the help we can get.

Finally, our reticence may indicate that we're just not that serious about dealing with a deeply imbedded sin. A willingness to come out of the closet (gays are not the only people wrestling with chronic problems) and set a goal with another person is an excellent way to show that we're in earnest about this. A reluctance to find a partner may tell you something important about your own half-hearted efforts.

Admitedly, some of us can't seem to find anyone we'd be comfortable sharing with. Some are much more isolated than others. But that's all the more reason to reach out and find someone somewhere—maybe even long-distance. Regular phone calls or letters can be a great source of encouragement, accountability, and stability.

And you'd be surprised at what you can turn up close by. The most bland, unassuming church-goer can often grow into a real encourager if given half a chance. Your opening up and sharing a need is often just the nudge someone needs to open up himself and join in the fight. So make some waves in your little corner of Christ's church. Drop a little honesty into the smooth, glassy surface of pleasant smiles and small talk in the sanctuary foyer. Watch the ripples spread.

One Sabbath day I listened groggily as our pastor rhapsodized at great length about the value of small-group interaction. He kept commending this kind of fellowship to our white, suburban, comfortable congregation and I, slouching in a back pew, kept retorting privately, "Yea, yea, more words. Where's the action? Why don't you just *do it*?"

A week later the pastor unveiled his plan for starting small groups within the church and invited all to join one. I had to eat my retort; I also had to join a group.

My wife and I met at a friend's house with other couples about our age and the pastor led us through exercises in sharing about ourselves and encouraging each other. During the next several weeks I watched us ordinary, unexciting church members become a body of Christ, a living organism. It was amazing what came out of these people you had greeted every week for years with the usual clichés. And it was remarkable how easily we were able to express genuine love and encouragement once we had committed ourselves to the group. It brought to mind the old college days with Campus Crusade for Christ when I'd been in an Action Group and felt so spiritually alive. I never thought that experience could be repeated. But there we were on those deep sofas — middle-aged bellies, worries about the kids, mortgages, bank accounts, and all — finding out what it meant again to have partners in the pursuit.

# 10

# The Big Picture

It HAD been a bad day in hell. The usual horrors faced by the men still fit enough to labor in the Auschwitz death camp had been compounded by yet another punishment. One starving prisoner had snitched a few potatoes and the authorities announced that either the guilty man be given up or the whole camp starve for a day. The twenty-five hundred living skeletons chose to fast.

That night as the men lay exhausted in their crude barracks, everyone felt the communal gloom. They were especially edgy and irritable. Then the lone light bulb burned out. Tempers flared. The senior block warden realized his charges were all on the verge of physical and emotional collapse; they desperately needed some kind of lift. So he asked a young Viennese physician named Viktor Frankl to give a talk.

Dr. Frankl was as cold and hungry, as jittery and tired as the rest of them. It took great effort to think of something encouraging. What could possibly be said to these dark, gaunt faces with hollow eyes? They'd become the playthings of capricious fate, digits in a frozen landscape ruled by moody, brutal guards. He remembered the day a group of sick men had to be transported to another camp. Several prisoners had to pile the emaciated bodies on two-wheeled carts. If one of the sick died before the carts departed he was thrown on anyway; the list had to be correct. Dead or alive, one's number was the important thing.

But Dr. Frankl also recalled that he'd seen more at Auschwitz than numbing inhumanity. Even here people made choices, little choices every day, which determined what one became — mentally and spiritually. Some managed generous gestures, sharing meager rations with the critically ill. He had been struck by "the depth and vigor of religious belief" in camp. Bone-tired, freezing men locked in the darkness of a cattle truck on the way back from a work site would gather in a corner to offer prayers. Frankl remembered how profoundly a beautiful sunset glimpsed through the dark clouds reverberated in the soul, and how devotedly one clung to the images of loved ones.

He'd come to believe that those who survived best in the camp seemed to nurture a "spiritual freedom — which cannot be taken away — that makes life meaningful and purposeful."

And so Dr. Frankl began speaking to his comrades about the key to survival. He forced out phrases which pried meaning from the spiritual tundra of that camp: *My chances may be slim, but I have no intention of losing hope and giving up. Whatever we have gone through can still be an asset in the future. All that we've experienced before life here is still with us. That is not lost. We have opportunities to give life meaning. Someone we love looks down on us and hopes to find us suffering proudly. We can always die for something.*

At the end of his talk, the light bulb flared up again and he made out "the miserable figures of my friends limping toward me to thank me with tears in their eyes."

After the war, Viktor Frankl used the insights he'd gained at Auschwitz to create a philosophy and practice of healing called "logotherapy." Other thinkers and psychiatrists had posited a will-to-power or will-to-pleasure as the driving force in human life. Dr. Frankl concluded that a will-to-meaning is fundamental to human change and psychological health. To "actualize himself" the individual needs more than just self-expression, finding out what's inside. "The meaning which a being has to fulfill," Frankl wrote, "is something beyond himself, it is never just himself."

What Viktor Frankl found to be essential in surviving the harsh imprisonment of Auschwitz, we will find very helpful in escaping the constraints of a habit. Meaning can be a great ally for change. It's yet another resource which gives momentum to a new behavior. And Christian believers have a lot of meaning to draw on.

## Laborer vs. Artist

In chapter eight we talked about digging down into our thoughts to try to get at troublesome and untrue assumptions. We tried to clarify and affirm specific beliefs. Now we need to step back a bit and look at a wider view. The big picture can motivate us for the long run.

Sometimes we burn out trying to churn a certain behavior out of our unwieldy human nature. But perspective can revive us. It helps to see our particular virtue-objective as something that expresses a larger truth. That is, our desired behavior is not just a mute, isolated deed, but something that speaks, that has cosmic reverberations.

This is the difference between functioning as a laborer and functioning as a craftsman or artist. The laborer sees only the work required of him; he goes through certain motions (often boring and repetitive ones) and gets paid after putting in a certain amount of time. The craftsman may go through very similar motions, and put in an equal amount of time, but he's driven by a desire to express something through his work. Similarly, the artist, traditionally at least, sees more than just putting a certain amount of paint on canvas. He's motivated to say something through color and shape and line. He's not just a painter covering surfaces for wages.

In our quest for change, a key factor for success is that we approach our task as an artist and not merely a laborer. Our acts of virtue are not just required motions that add up to a certain amount of merit. They can express something beautiful and profound, just as canvases do. Changing habits is not easy; we have to work at it. But if we see great meaning in our work, it will make all the difference, just as finding a meaning for their suffering made all the difference for Dr. Frankl and his fellow survivors.

Let's look at some examples of how specific virtues fit into the Big Picture.

## Divine Longsuffering

You want to replace blowing up with praising God. More importantly, you want to supplant the habit of impatience with the skill of malleability. What does that particular virtue express?

Paul once caught a glimpse of divine longsuffering expressed forcefully in his life. He describes it in his first letter to Timothy: "I was shown mercy so that in me, the worst of sinners, Christ Jesus might display His unlimited patience as an example for those who would believe. . . ." Christ is pictured as displaying or expressing His quality of merciful patience on the canvas of human life.

That divine quality seeks an echo within us. Part of the praise we may give is with our lives, expressing through our action the divine longsuffering that has meant so much to us. We express God's eternal faithfulness by the skill of malleability. We echo something of His character.

God is not caught in the flux, tripped up by the abrasive details; He resides in the slipstream of eternity. For Him a thousand years and one day are somehow interchangeable. He doesn't blow His stack when the toast gets burned or someone is late for an appointment. He dwells in immortal light. This is what we are privileged to express with our individual, tiny acts of patience and malleability. We have this treasure in earthen vessels, but it is treasure. We may not have spectacular successes all the time, but our every effort speaks to that grand and glorious theme: God's patience, His eternal forbearance.

Because God exists and because of who He is, our expressions of a virtue are never lost in the cracks and corners of life, however unnoticed they may appear to be. Every righteous act, like a daub of paint on the canvas, adds to the glory of God; it fills out the picture. We have a unique role to play on this planet which no one has had before in the history of the universe and no one else will again. We are called to reflect God's character in the midst of a world shattered by sin; we're called to embody truth in the place where it is distorted most horribly.

Our growth in Christ can be driven by a will-to-meaning. Every time we are moved by the Spirit to express a part of the divine nature, Satan the accuser is intimidated, his alternative empire of sin is shown to be a sham, and the watching universe bears witness to the power of God to wrest beauty from the jaws of disaster.

So rejoice in that. Whenever we take some step of malleability we move beyond the flux, we touch eternity.

## Healing Touch

You're working at replacing a habit of lust with solid sensitivity. That quality is also part of a bigger picture. What in particular does it reflect? A certain aspect of Jesus' ministry comes to mind: His surgically precise way of dealing with a whole spectrum of needs. I see solid sensitivity most of all as something which expresses Christ's healing touch.

Suddenly, the spectacle of a leper cuts a swath of horror through the crowd pressing close to the Master. They can see only rotting flesh and the pall of that most dreaded word, "Unclean." But Jesus sees more. He touches the leper. Yes, He is quite willing to make him clean. The Master wills ruddy health out of decay like a sculptor working angels from formless stone.

A beggar by the side of the road who had been born blind gets the same treatment. One touch. Cornea, retina, gelatin, rods, cones, optic nerve — all the tissues which had never cooperated before suddenly get together and produce the mystery of perfect vision. Christ's touch goes deep.

While mobbed in Capernaum as the healing celebrity, Jesus senses one fleeting touch unlike all the others pressing against His flesh. A woman who had suffered from internal bleeding for twelve years has made a desperate gesture. Jesus stops the momentum of the town cold in order to recognize her, refocus superstition to faith, and extend His healing hand.

Christ's touch was exact, sensitive, piercing to the marrow. It created wholeness where there were only scars, lesions, and pain. This is what our acts of solid sensitivity can express. Our getting below the surface embodies His penetrating regard. Our encouraging the neglected manifests His hopeful eye.

The struggle to get beyond sexual stimuli and reach some inner worth in our neighbors is not just an isolated act of propriety. It's part of the gracious regard of Christ. Our acts of solid sensitivity express something with divine resonance. We are privileged to brush on a few strokes depicting the Master who never got lost in the external accidents of the flesh but always reached toward the innermost heart.

## Bits of the Creator

Thankfulness, that worthy adversary of habitual depression, also has its divine reverberations. What are we really doing when we pause in our work to give thanks, when we decipher the blessings through the daily grind? The most obvious thing this expresses is that there is a God up there to be thankful to. But it also can speak of Him in particular — as the Creator. It says life is created, purposive, as opposed to merely a random tumbling through time. Thankfulness says that the good in life is what is going to last forever, and evil a temporary aberration. So why get fixed on the bad? Why freeze in its atmosphere? We bear witness to what is ultimate when we look through the sharp pain or plain monotony around us and fix on blessings—bits of the Creator still floating around in our world, not yet consumed by sin.

   If disaster and randomness were really the fundamental state of the universe, then thankfulness could be seen as merely wishful thinking, a refusal to see life as it is. But God has woven meaning into His creation; it still pops through the most ordinary days, the loneliest nights. Our calling is to catch it, brush the dirt off, and let it shine. Signs of the Creator which we uncover are like the artifacts an archeologist digs up which tell tales of a culture some distance removed from us, but very real.

## The Interceding Lord

   How about resentment and its counterpoint, sharp mercy? You've begun to pray for the person who irritates you in order to express a virtue and exclude a bad habit. What does that say? Acts of sharp mercy are more than just the required square pegs to fit the square holes of righteousness. They suggest a larger picture of God Himself, the One who intercedes for the unworthy.

   That is the transcendant fact we represent by our own small acts of intercession. We echo our interceding Lord— Christ spending all night on the hills above Lake Galilee praying for His slow-of-heart disciples, pleading for those who were often His heaviest burden. Jesus in the Garden of Gethsemane concerned about His three snoring friends whose flesh was weak—while all hell was breaking loose around Him. This is the divine meaning we may make plain to the world. Even hot-tempered Moses added a compelling scene to the great canvas of intercession when he cried out for forty days: "Blot my name out of your book, but please forgive your people, accept them again."

   We embody a piece of divine intercession every time we pray for obnoxious Susan. Such acts help us know more intimately what makes the God of the universe tick. He wants us to share in His own holiness, not just some distantly related imitation. He permits us to feel something of what it's like to be God. Remember that fact when you're at the office trying to say a few good words to the Lord on behalf of the one who wronged you again. You're not just one isolated believer nudging out a righteous act that trickles away unnoticed. You're part of the Big Picture. You, too, can put a few strokes of color on the canvas of divine mercy.

## The Biggest Picture

As we see our individual virtue-objectives take on a larger significance because of what they express about God and His truth, we'll be able to see our Christian walk as a whole in a broader light. A great deal of New Testament teaching magnifies the meaning of following Christ, it sets the struggle in a glorious setting. This perspective can move us far beyond any inhibiting sense that we're just eeking out a moral existence to fulfill obligations, racking up a few more points in the dreary trek toward sanctification.

Scripture communicates the pursuit of virtue as a great ambition, a highest calling that consumes our greatest energies. The New Testament writers saw themselves as part of a dynamic, irresistible movement of grace which sets people free.

Unforgettable scenes on the nightly news in late 1989 gave us a glimpse of what a movement of people in pursuit of an ideal can really mean. Thousands of candles lit up the night in Budapest as Hungarians commemorated the 1956 uprising against Soviet rule. East Germans massed around railroad tracks to cheer on a train overflowing with those who had left all for freedom. A mass of clenched fists and victory signs rose in the night streets of Prague. A group of believers linking their arms around the Reformed Church in Timiosaura, Romania, confronted Ceaucescu's Securiate forces. In Sofia, Bulgaria exultant demonstrators chanted democracy slogans hour after hour until their communist world cracked open.

The West watched in wonder as the citizens of Eastern Europe changed history by marching in the streets. Their voices of protest against repressive regimes united into a great chorus of freedom; the banners and flags waved above their heads coalesced into a formidable statement and these brave souls became an irresistible movement of destiny.

As believers we are all part of a movement for freedom. Paul urges us to man the barricades lifted up against Satan's repressive empire, wave our white banner of the pure gospel, and stand firm in the freedom to which Christ calls us. The minute we confront some chronic sin in our lives and aim to replace it with a quality in Christ, we have stepped out into the streets; we've challenged the evil empire. Our struggles with habits may be frustrating and seem insignificant, but they put us *in* the race; we start marching in a movement; our frail voice unites in a great chorus of freedom. God wants each of us to find individual meaning as part of this great movement, this historic march out of one age and into another.

Bright New Testament passages urge us on. Forgetting the moral litter strewn behind us we press ahead toward a high and heavenly calling, swept along as trophies in Christ's triumphant procession. We run with the Spirit in our hearts as a pledge of great things to come, fixing our eyes on Christ the author and perfector of our faith. We are the fragrance of Christ sent out into the world. We're surrounded by a cheering cloud of witnesses who've laid down heroic deeds before us; we fight successfully against principalities and powers of darkness. We join the most important race with our eyes on the greatest prize.

Never forget the biggest picture. Don't let your singular struggle on this singular day overshadow the great highway on which you travel. Don't let any failure blot out the heavenly challenge which has laid hold of you. Thank God every day that you can be part of the good fight of faith, becoming a participant in the very nature of God Himself.

# Summary: Resources

The four preceding chapters explored additional resources which play a supportive role in our efforts to replace a habit and which keep us moving in the right direction.

Chapter 7 dealt with our emotions.

**Up and down moods**
*Don't aim at emotions; aim at God.*
*Learn to praise creatively.*
**Lack of momentum**
*Personal discoveries stimulate change.*
*Claim a spirit of wisdom and revelation.*

Chapter 8 presented a strategy for wielding our beliefs.

**Hidden assumptions**
*Bring implicit beliefs out into the light.*
*Expose the lie with scriptural statements.*
*Affirm the truth loud and clear: what you do believe.*

Chapter 9 explained why we seek a partner in the pursuit.

**Encouragement**
Specific sharing about a common goal.
**Accountability**
Light shed on each other's blind spots.
**Consistency**
One is strong when the other is weak.

Chapter 10 recommended the perspective of the big picture.

### Meaning is a great ally

*Your isolated actions echo a larger truth.*
*Reflect on what your counterpoint virtue expresses about God.*

### The highest calling

*Participate in the nature of God Himself.*
*Join the historic march out of one age and into another.*

As part of the rewriting of the Spirit within us, these four scripts form still more expanding circles in our minds. Though they overlap to some extent, each one centers around different personal territory (see figure 10).

Our rewriting related to emotions employs the steady gaze of praise and the spirit of revelation to create more and more room for both stability and momentum. As a result, moodiness and emotional inertia disrupt our progress less and less.

Rewriting our assumptions allows God's truth to etch in deeper lines than those irrational self-statements which keep dragging us back to the habit.

The experience of sharing with a partner in the pursuit removes the weapon of secrecy from the hands of the enemy, illuminating those blind spots that can blindside us.

Seeing what our counterpoint virtue expresses about God magnifies our individual struggle into a more meaningful quest; we no longer act merely as laborers putting in time, but as artists and craftsmen giving glory to the Father.

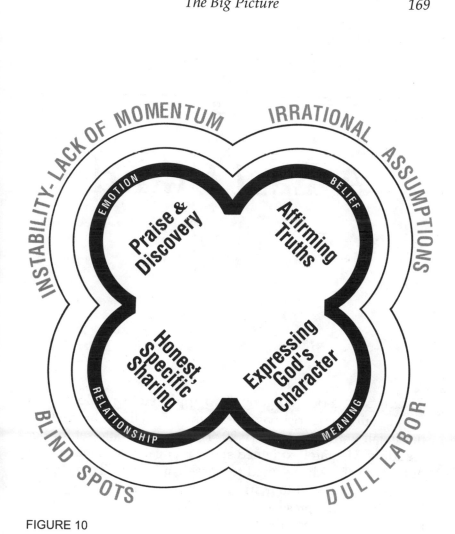

FIGURE 10

# 11

# A Last Stand

SEVENTEEN-YEAR-OLD Margaret Caro appeared in a Colorado juvenile court one Christmas season and asked the judge to place her in jail until after January 20. That was the date set for her wedding. Margaret explained she was engaged to a man much older than she who seemed to possess a mesmerizing charm. The girl didn't want to marry him, but she just couldn't resist him while in his presence. So she pleaded for a short stay in jail in order to "break the spell."

The judge reluctantly consented. After a few weeks Margaret emerged from her cell beaming. "Just as I expected," she said, "I'm cured—no wedding bells for me!"

Most of us chuckle or harrumph at this extraordinarily vulnerable individual. But in our hassles with the Big Habit there are times we operate on her premises, believing that once the enemy breaks through our defenses and confronts us face-to-face, we're helpless; there's nothing to do but give in.

## The Last Weapon

I do remember certain unpleasant occasions, like old bruises on my limbs which still ache, when I exposed myself as sitting duck. Like the time the enemy had pretty well broken through all my circles of offense. A tight schedule and late nights had crunched my quiet time into a paltry, token gesture. I'd slipped into a rather numb statement of the will and lingered lethargically on Satan's ground. No battle cries in sight. My witness for the prosecution sat down tongue-tied.

Now temptation crashed through right in my face. The heat was on and I could taste the sin. Feeling like a mouse in the cat's paw, I concluded, quite reasonably, that the battle had already been lost. I'd walked into the trap virtually disarmed since I'd spent almost no meaningful time in prayer or the Word. What was the point of fighting? My big mistake came early in the morning, that's when I should have fought. Besides, I mused, I've already soiled myself with evil thoughts and become a willing target. Why should I struggle when I know I'm going to lose? So I gave in—and determined that next time I would keep my circles of offense intact.

Some time later I realized that I'd created yet another trap to fall into: using previous shortcomings to excuse a present capitulation. My very proper emphasis on winning the battle early had subtly become a reason not to fight late. I'd assumed that I had no weapons left. But there is one last weapon that remains— even when temptation has wrapped its arms around us and we feel our soul wither. God asks us to do something difficult: "Resist the devil, and he will flee from you. Come near to God and He will come near to you. Wash your hands, you sinners, and purify your hearts, you double-minded" ( James 4:7–8).

You're already a sinner. You've already got your hands dirty anticipating the kick of sin. You're pathetically double-minded, head saturated with resentment or anger or adulterous lust, and only a few stray thoughts darting toward heaven. Okay, but you can still do something about it. You can wash your hands, as Scripture says. You can purify your heart.

You should never have allowed yourself to get in a position where the devil can intimidate you. True. You should never
have cozied up to the temptations of the evil one. Right. But if
you do find him pressing close, you can still resist. When
temptation breaks through several lines of defense, don't be
afraid to duke it out, don't give up just because you lost the
first few rounds. The devil may be roaring like a lion in your
face, but "Resist him, standing firm in the faith. . . ."

Our final resource, the last tower in our overrun fortress,
is to resist. It's basic grunt-work, saying no through our teeth,
hanging on a few more minutes. Here are some good reasons
for wielding our last weapon.

## There's a Way Out (of Even This)

We resist primarily because God has promised that our predicament is not hopeless. Jesus Christ Himself felt the heat, the
fury of Satan up close. He agonized. Hebrews 2:18 tells us "Because he himself suffered when he was tempted, he is able to
help those who are being tempted." God is not an ivory-tower
general shouting down instructions to us poor mortals writh-
ing in the mud of temptation. He has been down suffering under the pressure of sin. So He is able to urge us on and fight
with us — even in the thick of ugly battle.

Paul makes the promise crystal clear: "And God is faithful; He will not let you be tempted beyond what you can bear.
But when you are tempted, He will also provide a way out so
that you can stand up under it" (1 Corinthians 10:13). There
are times when you feel the pressure is just too much. Your
carnal nature is locked into some sin like a pit bull with an
ankle in its jaws. There seems no way out of this overwhelming temptation, and you can't survive another second in its
oppressive atmosphere. But God says, "Wait, look around;
there's an exit. I can enable you to stand — even in the fire.

"Even the captives of the mighty will be taken away,
And the prey of the tyrant will be rescued;
For I will contend with the one who contends with you,
And I will save your sons" (Isaiah 49:25).

I remember distinctly one occasion in which "the flesh" had me up against the wall. Temptation had attracted, bemused, and saturated my thoughts. I was on the edge of giving in to the old porn routine.

It's all but impossible to extricate yourself once you've been sucked in that deeply. Once the enticement has you fixed, there's only one way out: *do it*. But this time I managed one last token gesture of resistance. I opened my Bible to Romans 8. Praying with desperate half-heartedness, I tried to read. I called on the Mighty God to deliver me. (It's hard to do that while savoring sin at the same time.)

Somehow those familiar words of Paul about new life in the Spirit caught hold. I prayed more wholeheartedly. I continued to read, and then—my mind switched gears. Thoughts hopelessly locked into lust bounced up to spiritual themes. God's principles became exciting; I could expand in them.

And so I was freed. Right there in the same environment that had made me so vulnerable. Right there with the same sin available. I had been strengthened in the inner man and could resist. I resisted, in fact, rather jubilantly.

There *is* a way out. Sparks of life fly your way as you resist. When you feel sin pulling hard, then "lift up your drooping hands and strengthen your weak knees, and make straight paths for your feet, so that the limb which is lame may not be put out of joint, but rather be healed." We may be limping along under the assaults of the enemy, drooping under the weight of temptation; we may think we're so close to sin we might as well fall altogether—but God encourages us to make a last stand; there's still value in resisting. It's one thing to be lame, quite another to dislocate a bone, so start mending those limbs.

## Confronting the Tyranny of Now

Another important reason to resist is that we must all at some point face up to the tyranny of now. Chronic sin jerks us around because it can aways count on a big push from the present momentary pleasure, the present venting of ugly feelings, the present wallowing in worry or self-pity. Almost all habits are

habits because of the dictatorship of this moment, the irresistible command. We know all about the benefits of later; we know
very well what is best in the long run. It's the benefit of *now*
that gets us. It's always this temporary, forgivable detour that
pulls us back into trouble. As psychologist Rodger K. Bufford
explained: "Choosing to be thin next week rather than to eat
candy next week poses no problem. The difficulty occurs when
we must choose between eating candy now and being thin next
week. . . ." Oscar Wilde put it more simply: "I can resist anything except temptation."

The tyranny of now gives us a great alibi: "It wasn't really
me; I just couldn't help myself." But we have to face the fact
that moral failures never happen in a vacuum. There's always a
"reason" for sin. Any kind of healthy, righteous life is going to
have to be built against the grain. A little resistance when sin
looms large can go a long way toward molding character.

So we must remain present and accounted for during
those moments of weakness. We can't always expect to deal
with sin from a great distance. There will be occasions when
we have to make a hard choice between feeling good now and
being satisfied in the Lord later. If we only maintain our aim at
virtue as long as temptation doesn't get too close, then the tyranny of now will remain the devil's ace in the hole. He'll know
we can be had every time our preventative strategy of spending time in the Word breaks down a bit. Sometimes the act of
resistance (even with our hands dirty) is our clearest moral
deed, since it confronts the essence of the sin problem and de-
nies its loudest claims.

Centuries ago, during the long and brutal persecution of
the French Huguenots, a Spanish force was besieging the town
of St. Quentin, where the Protestants had taken refuge. Things
looked grim. The city's ramparts were broken down; famine
and fever had cut down the ranks of the defenders; there was
talk of treason among the terrified population.

One day the Spaniards sent a shower of arrows over the
walls to which were attached slips of parchment. The messages
stated that if the inhabitants would surrender, their lives and

property would be spared. The leader of the Huguenots, Gaspard de Coligni, wrote his own message on a piece of parchment, tied it to a javelin, and had it thrown back to the besiegers. His reply consisted of two words: "Regem habemus" (We have a king).

A resolve to defy the dictatorship of the present moment declares our fundamental allegiance. Even when bullied and bruised and about to give up, we can say, "Yes, right now, I have a King."

## Acquiring Hard Victories

Finally, we resist because there is nothing quite as uplifting as having won a difficult fight. To be able to say, "I've taken the worst the adversary can dish out and still, in God's strength, come out unvanquished" — that's something to have in the bank. It's a great weapon to hold against a pernicious habit. You know you've gone that far; you've created new territory in which to stand firm.

On a Monday night in Paris, I lay in bed from midnight to five totally exhausted and wide awake. We'd come over to tape segments for a television series. I was laboring with a case of industrial strength jet lag, feeling miserable there in the stuffy darkness of a hotel room, dead tired after racing around the city all day — and not a wink to show for it.

In the dead of that night temptation rushed over me. In this case pornography was the drawing card — so close, down by the lobby. I'd been nicely set up hours before as I flipped through French TV and caught those body parts sizzling on channel one. Only the quick-cutting camera style saved me from going breathless to indulgent. Now the enemy pressed hard. I fought back earnestly and feebly, trying to remember that I had an eight-month clean record on my hands. Burying my head in the pillow, I cried to God against the heat, "Save me, save me, just give me sleep. Just put me out of my misery." I grabbed onto that thought: "I can't make it — You've got to save me. Put me to sleep."

But sleep didn't fall from heaven. I had to lay there wretchedly awake, growing weaker and weaker from the continual yanks of the enemy. *After all, it's such a forgivable sin. What's a little slick, white-collar porn going to harm?*

I was getting pretty upset with the Lord. How long was this going to go on? Sleep, I thought, was the least He could do for me. But then another thought struck with some force: *This is the time to fight altogether. Now, at a moment of greatest weakness, is the opportunity to establish some real resistance, to erect a barrier deep in enemy territory. I've succumbed to fantasy; I've been dragged down already; I'm physically exhausted and about to come unglued because I can't sleep. The battle seems over. Now is the chance to make a historic stand.*

That grim yet promising idea rang true. So I prayed out a vow: "Come what may, Lord, sin is not an option. I'll worship all night in gloom; I'll stay in Your arms. No demands that blessing precede or promote victory. No laying down conditions for my obeying Your law. If You don't show favor, I'm not going to sin. To resist in Christ's name is reward enough."

I thought my belated show of bravery would collapse any minute. But I continued talking to God, not just to myself, and it held up. Although the old bullying temptation kept making passes at me through the night, I managed to grunt out a dirty, groggy "no."

Morning did come at last. I enjoyed a good breakfast and had the privilege of thanking God for a hard victory. The Victorious Warrior and I had erected a barricade of great value and claimed new territory.

### Talking Back

We've looked at why we can and should resist in moments of weakness. We've put on a game face and prepared for heavy action by acknowledging there's a way out, by choosing to confront the tyranny of now, and by seeing the value of hard victories. Is there anything we can say about *how* to resist?

Scripture suggests no magic techniques or guaranteed formulas here. As I said before, this is simple grunt work. But we do have one method of using a very powerful tool. To resist the devil in our face, we throw the Word at him as fast as we can. That's what Christ did when Satan ambushed Him in a desolate wilderness and fired off his three best shots.

In a previous chapter, I explained why you want to avoid getting into hand-to-hand combat with transgression if at all possible. You don't need to get tangled up in arguments with the enemy. Our strategy is to overwhelm temptations with the Word as soon as we see the whites of their eyes.

But now we're talking about an emergency, our last recourse. If your expanding circles have collapsed, and the enemy is breathing down your neck, then do talk back to him. Resist. Rebuke in Christ's name.

For example, say the roaring lion comes with his favorite quip: "Do it *now*."

You shoot back: "I tell you now is the time of God's favor, now is the day of salvation."

He persists, "Come on, it's no biggie."

You reply, "Who are you kidding? 'Can a man scoop fire into his lap without his clothes being burned?'"

"I suppose it's going to kill you."

"Evil desires wage 'war against the soul.'"

"But think about it, wouldn't it be nice. . . ."

"I'll stand with Moses who 'chose to be mistreated along with the people of God rather than to enjoy the pleasures of sin for a short time.'"

"You're all by yourself, fool. No one's going to know. Why be miserable?"

"I rebuke you in Christ name. I resist 'firm in the faith' knowing that my 'brothers throughout the world are undergoing the same kind of sufferings.'"

The point, of course, is not to get into an extended dia-
logue. Do your best to tell Satan, "Away from me!" and mean
it. The only reason you're talking is that you find yourself
entangled in the temptation and about to succumb. As quickly
as you can, turn your prayer to the positive, to God Himself.

That's how you resist in the thick of it. The three 'whys'
of resisting, the good reasons, should get you to the point of
using the Word. As soon as you're willing, start talking back
with combative Bible verses as vigorously as possible. If you
can just keep doing that for a bit, Scripture itself will rescue
you. Remember its double-edged sharpness as the sword of
the Spirit; it can cut a way of escape through the most
belligerent, encircling temptations.

## With All Our Strength

Hard victories are a great thing to have, but if you find
yourself regularly having to resist while temptation bends you
over backwards, then something's wrong. Wrestling in prayer
with God's Word is the preferred exercise. Check your other
resources; check your circles of offense. Are you building them
up or allowing them to decay? You've got to win the battle
much earlier as a rule.

Also, don't be devastated if you do lose in close combat
most of the time. Unless you have extraordinary willpower,
you won't make much progress fighting hand-to-hand. Just
learn to celebrate whatever hard victories you can scrape out
by God's grace. Rejoice in what you have accomplished much
more than sorrow over where you've failed.

There are exceptions, though. Let's say you've gotten in
the habit of robbing banks. You become a Christian and set up
your strategy to replace that sin. You grow strong in the rich-
ness of the Word. But of course once in a while your devotional
life trickles away and you find yourself "out of the Spirit."
Hitting First Interstate seems like a wonderful idea. If you do
slip back into the act, however, it will be pretty hard to excuse.

It's tough explaining, "I know I robbed a bank the other day, but I just didn't have a good quiet time."

Habits involving deliberate, premeditated acts which hurt other people require 100 percent elimination more urgently than less damaging character flaws. Resisting the temptation to rob banks *most of the time* when that temptation strikes hard won't do much for your Christian experience. Being faithful to your spouse *almost* all the time isn't something to memorialize either. It's a little like locking almost all your car doors in a bad neighborhood.

The same applies even more to physically addictive habits. One slip very easily plunges us back into complete dependency again. Any deeply rooted habit never completely surrenders its claims on us. We remain recovering — not recovered — sinners, clinging to grace each day of our lives. I had to reach the point where I evaluated being completely "clean" from pornography in terms of years, one year at a time. I realize that one bad slip can send me back into the old addictive pattern.

But thank God that even in the roughest times, we do have that final resource, that desperate flinging of the Word, which can result in remarkable victories.

Someone overheard a small boy declare that he loved his mother "with all my strength," and asked him what he meant. The boy replied, "Well, we live on the fourth floor of this place, and there's no elevator, and they keep the coal down in the basement. Mother's busy all the time and she isn't very strong, so I see to it that the coal hold is never empty. I lug the coal up the stairs all by myself. It takes all my might to get it up there. Isn't that loving her with all my strength?"

Resisting all the way — when our resources seem about as potent as a little kid struggling with a load of black coal — is one way we can love God with all our strength and heart and mind.

# 12

# Putting It All Together

Listen to the war stories of those who've wrestled at some length with habits and you'll soon pick up a common refrain: the fear of being one step away from disaster. People with sad, weary faces tell each other, "Temptation always comes at your weakest moments." "If you let down your guard in just one area, it's all over." "The devil has so many ways of coming at you."

I think it's about time we came back at him. Each preceding chapter has given us a different way of countering the enemy, of creating layers of offense. I've tried to present an alternative to our traditional laments. We need to see powerful resources all around us instead of just deadly temptations. By rewriting with the Word, by setting up our expansive circles, we establish the rules of the game and so cease being maneuvered into a defensive posture. We make temptation multiply our weapons and the threat of habitual sin push us into a more intense and fruitful devotional life. Instead of slip-sliding away under the constant pressure, we apply the pressure. Satan must challenge us on our ground, on God's ground, on God's terms.

This strategy allows us to deal with chronic sin seriously and yet remain positive and well-balanced human beings. Every circle is a means of growth, something we can continue over the long haul. This is a kind of fight we can live with; it's the best way I know to keep from burning out in the struggle for righteousness. Here are the the key reasons why.

## The Spice of Variety

A lot of people drop out of the good fight because they wear out a single weapon. We may get excited about praise, for example, as a way to deal with the enemy. So we start praising away under temptation. That's a good weapon and it can take you some distance, but after a while, praise alone starts to fray around the edges. We're repeating the same old phrases. We've done it all before. Our discoveries in this one area trickle out and adoration increasing falls flat.

It's very difficult to wield one weapon over and over again and remain successful. It's not that praise itself becomes impotent, but our hold on it loosens; repetition numbs our grip. And so we come to believe that praise just doesn't work anymore.

If we want to fight successfully we need a whole arsenal. Different weapons tend to utilize different spiritual muscles. It's best to distribute the exercise to our whole body so we don't exhaust ourselves in one particular way of fighting. Some people relate to chronic sin only in terms of resisting. Resistance is a great weapon, but you get worn out on it. A life of withstanding temptation burns people out. We need other lighter weapons to call on for support.

Some of us major exclusively in our identity with Christ. We concentrate on a positive image of who we are and believe such a perspective will determine what we do. Focusing on our identity with Christ is a great weapon. But our eyes blurr after a while, trying to fix on that one truth. We can't keep it up. Taking good aim at a virtue, picking up a few battle cries, reinforcing counterpoint behavior — these weapons are necessary too.

We need variety for the long haul. If we're serious about overcoming deeply imbedded habits, then we need to think in terms of a healthy way of life, not just spurts of effort with one spiritual instrument we get excited about for a few weeks. Confessing, identifying with Christ, aiming at virtue, expressing that virtue, arming ourselves to the teeth, praising God, consciously affirming the truth — all these strategies are healthy, fruitful things to do, regardless of what sin we're struggling with. They have value in themselves, not just in their capacity to oppose evil.

And they are open-ended, expansive circles. We don't just dig trenches and fight off the assaults of the enemy. That is precisely the picture of the virtuous life that secular people find so forbidding. No, we don't just try to defend our turf. We're expanding. We're finding more to praise, more solidarity to claim, more virtue to flesh out, more statements to make in the world, more meaning to affirm.

Our expansive circles are skills to develop. Good for a lifetime. We're knocking all the props out from under the old habit and building all kinds of props under a counterpoint virtue. Variety is the spice of the good life.

## Whole Human Beings

In the past, efforts to help people change have often centered on one particular piece of our selves. Freud, and the psychoanalysts who followed him, zeroed in on the subconscious. They believed they had discovered the key to unlocking all our secrets in those subterranean passages of the psyche. They built and re-built elaborate theories on how to take people apart and put them back together again. But later, other therapists got tired of digging in this labyrinth and decided to tackle our difficulties more directly. Behaviorists decided that our actions are the point where change is most significant. If you just modify behavior, then the subconscious, the emotions, the thought-patterns, will fall in line, or at least cease to be a problem.

Others disagreed. "Get in touch with your feelings" became the rallying cry for those who believed that changing our emotions is what changes everything else. Then the cognitive therapists came along and said, "Quit fiddling with all this vague emotional territory, just change people's thought patterns. If you get people to think straight, they will act straight and even begin to feel straight."

As a result of these competing theories, we've had endless chicken-and-egg debates among those in the counseling professions. Do emotions change thought-patterns, or do thought-patterns change emotions? Does new behavior transform our thoughts, or do new thoughts transform our behavior? Which comes first? Where is the best place to start? Lately, more and more therapies have tried to broaden their approaches and include strategies that deal with behavior, emotions, and cognitive processes. But most still emphasize one aspect of the self as the key to "real change."

What about Scripture — does it take sides? We have that often-quoted admonition about "renewing our minds" and verses which urge us to fill our thoughts with good things. But we also see emphasis on "what proceeds from the heart of man" and a divine interest in replacing hearts of stone with hearts of flesh. And there are also plenty of biblical calls for specific changes in behavior in the spirit of James' "blessed are the doers of the law" (the moral equivalent of "Just Do It").

Scripture advocates change in various ways on various levels. It aims at a healing of spirit, soul, and body. The important thing is that we deal with ourselves as whole human beings. Our emotions, our behavior, our thoughts, even our subconscious, are all part of what God has created. They are all interrelated. Behavior affects emotions. Emotions affect behavior. Thoughts determine behavior. Behavior determines thought patterns. It's all true. We're an undissectible whole. You can't just cut out a piece, try to manipulate it, and then stick it back in again. Every part of us affects every other part of us.

That's why this book presents a multi-layered strategy for change. We need to get the whole human system working on the side of the Spirit. Different people fall into unhealthy habits in different ways. Some get tangled up on an emotional level; that's the problem that dominates. Others are tripped up primarily by unhealthy behaviors. Still others present a jumble of counterproductive thought-patterns as the big hurdle. Different habits acquire their strongest support in different areas.

We may need to work on one particular expanding circle more than others. That's fine. The exact point where we start in the process of change is not as important as our goal of getting our whole selves involved with the whole of God's resources. We want to get to the point where emotion and behavior and thinking are reinforcing each other in the pursuit of a certain virtue.

## Taking Models Too Far

Two strategies for change have become prominent recently among two very different groups of people. Mental health professionals increasingly work through an addiction model of behavior, while Christians in the "deliverance movement" increasingly see all unhealthy behavior in terms of demon possession.

Addiction is an enormous problem these days; our society is full of substances that invite abuse. Those involved in extricating the victims and their families from these webs of addiction naturally develop theories of how people progress in and out of physical and psychological "attachment." And it becomes possible to interpret any problem behavior through that model. We start hearing of people addicted to pistachio nuts, sunbathing, being right, and reading the paper in the morning.

The model of addiction does provide a useful way of looking at all kinds of problems. But it can be carried too far. It has led some to see "attachment" or "dependence" itself as the problem. Anything which we are compelled to do, however noble the motive, anything which we are not totally free to drop, is an addiction. In other words, there are no good habits.

In this view, we don't replace an unhealthy behavior with anything else; that's just to create a "substitute addiction" in which all our compulsions are simply transferred to a new object. Instead, people are advised to just not do it and face the emptiness on the other side of addiction.

It's understandable that some mental health professionals would acquire such a perspective since they typically work with the more neurotic and psychotic among us. That's their data base. Disturbed people do tend to turn any pleasurable or rewarding activity into something compulsive. Attachments of all kinds carry perils.

But even for them, the main problem is not in liking something too much or finding some act wonderfully rewarding. It's simply whether we are fulfilling a healthy need in a healthy way or not. People can enjoy sunbathing immensely and want to do it every Friday and miss it if they don't — all for healthy reasons. Others can sunbathe once for unhealthy reasons.

In order to adopt new behaviors for good reasons we have to take care of basic needs related to guilt, identity, will. If we try to manufacture a good habit in order to take care of unresolved guilt, then an unhealthy attachment may develop. If we continue trying to change ourselves on our own, without Christ's will on our side, then we'll be frustrated. If we try to perform in order to create a secure identity, then "substitute addictions" are certainly possible.

Guilt, an ambivalent will, and a poor self-concept are bad motivators. Just tacking on a new behavior doesn't resolve these issues. That's why I started this book with the strategies of confession, making a stand at the cross, and identifying with Christ. These things do solve the problems and allow us to adopt healthy alternatives to bad habits.

Christians in the "deliverance ministry" interpret compulsive behavior in starkly different terms from those used in the addiction model. They're struggling to help people whose unhealthy behavior is often accompanied by paranormal phenomenon: jerking limbs, strange voices, bizarre thoughts that seem to originate elsewhere. Those who seek exorcism feel just as helpless as the drug addicts checking into a clinic.

I believe the demon possession model is useful in dealing with some very serious problems that carry overt signs of satanic activity. People have indeed been "delivered" from various compulsions when demons were cast out in the name of Jesus. But, again, this model can be carried too far. Christians accustomed to wrestling evil spirits under the lordship of Christ begin to see demons behind every human problem. Students who have trouble studying have been counseled to seek deliverance from the demon of inattention; lethargic housewives start seeing demonic attacks in every spell of boredom; some sneezing believers even try to cast out the common cold.

Throwing out every conceivable demon is not the key to successful living. Exorcism is just a first step out of compulsions, necessary in some cases, which must lead to growing in Christ, aiming at His qualities, affirming His truths. We don't want to keep the devil at the center of attention.

In confession, our honest and open agreement with God, we do make a break with those "principalities and powers," those "forces of darkness." We decisively sever all ties by making a stand at the cross, claiming the blood of Christ, and we further distance ourselves by becoming witnesses for the prosecution and taking up an unequivocal battle cry. All these strategies wreck havoc on the designs of the enemy.

I've tried to create a balance with the strategies in this book. We want to use the best from the behavioral principles of the addiction model and also take seriously the spiritual warfare emphasized by the deliverance people.

## Positive Change Process

The strategies presented in each chapter can be grouped

in three general levels. First we have the three core circles that deal with guilt, will, and identity. We have to first take care of business on that level in order to progress to behavior change. Honest confession, making a stand at the cross, and finding an identity in Christ set the stage for all that follows.

The next level focuses us on changing behavior. We replace the unhealthy habit by reinforcing counterpoint actions. Aiming at a virtue and arming ourselves to the teeth prepare us to throw out the old in order to welcome in the new.

At the outer level we have strategies which play a supportive role in changing behavior. Feelings, beliefs, meaning, and other people can all become allies, helping us to keep moving forward. They amplify the changes we have initiated.

Finally, we throw up an inner fortification, the circle of resistance, where we commit ourselves to make a last stand, if necessary (see figure 11).

Through the rewriting power of God's Word, these healthy scripts execute a positive and sustainable process of change. The arrows of the enemy are deflected off our expanding circles of offense and more room is created for our becoming new creatures in Christ.

## *One Verse At a Time*

Now that we've seen why we try to put it all together, let's look at how we put it all together. First of all, recognize that this is a long-term solution to a chronic problem; it's something that you build up over time. At first glance, this list of strategies can appear a bit intimidating—how on earth will we ever get it constructed? Don't feel that you must have all your expanding circles set up the first week, or that you have to work on each circle every day.

You build the system up a single step at a time. One day you might find something in your Scripture reading that makes a great battle cry. The next day you may run across a verse that sheds light on Christ's sacrificial stand at Calvary. Thank God for it; write it down; meditate on it; stake your claim to it; add it to your arsenal. The rewriting of our minds happens one

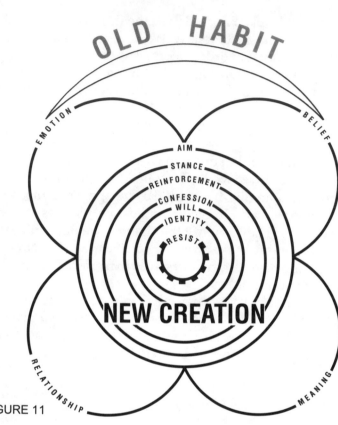

FIGURE 11

verse at a time, one discovery at a time. This many-layered strategy gives you a way to organize the Word for action. You are
building up a coherent spiritual edifice around you instead of
just picking up bits of inspiration at random.

Keeping a notebook helps a lot. Devote a few pages to
each of your weapon-resources, with headings like:

- Good Confession
- Standing at the Cross
- Identified with Christ
- My Hidden Treasure

- Battle Cries
- Fleshing Out This Virtue
- Praise Paraphrase
- What I Believe

Then begin to write in Bible verses you discover that
apply to each circle of offense. Slowly you'll see your arsenal

built up; you'll see God's Word take definite and creative shape. This is an important visual cue. It helps make apparent in your own mind just how you are replacing an old habit with a new virtue. The notebook will also keep those weapons within reach as you review them regularly. Use it in your daily prayer; now you have something positive and purposive to lift up to God instead of just a vague plea for help. You come before the throne of grace propelled by Scripture.

These verses are like troop companies deployed around a particular circle. You activate that circle by prayerfully filling it with Scripture. Again, you may not have all your troops alert at every single circle, every single day. But you're constantly building up strength at various points. By continuing to apply verses in very specific ways, you constantly open up new fronts against the enemy. Here a counterpoint virtue springs to life, there a confession is given new earnestness, and over there a discovery in praise springs up. You're on the offensive. You keep the enemy off balance. He doesn't know where the Word may strike next. Reinforcements keep pouring into the circles; the circles keep expanding.

It's not really a complicated strategy. It just requires a steady pace, a few steps at a time. After a while you may indeed be able to blaze away on several fronts at once. You'll have passages of Scripture established very clearly as weapons and be able to send out a real barrage that overwhelms the habit.

## No Surrender

Although you won't be able to build up every weapon every day, do remember this: don't sell out on any line of offense. Some of us may have a particularly hard time with hidden assumptions, others with fickle emotions or a compulsive behavior. There may come a time when you feel like giving up in one particular area and just moving on to something else. Don't grant the devil a toehold. You may have a struggle, that circle may break up repeatedly, but don't abandon it. Keep bringing reinforcements. Keep challenging the lie with the power of the Word. Remember that God has a knack for manifesting His strength through our weakness. He may inspire you to make your greatest stand at your point of greatest frailty.

But even if this area of struggle remains a source of vul- nerability, your other expansive circles will lend support and help protect it—as long as you don't forsake your efforts there. In other words, you may be much better at praise than at resisting, or you may find that aiming at a virtue comes much easier than making a stand at the cross. Fine, excel in praise; aim wholeheartedly at a virtue. But also be willing to resist sin, be willing to make a stand, and don't neglect to absorb Scripture toward that end. We can compensate for a weakness, but a gaping hole invites defeat.

## The Classic Spiritual Discipline

All of this, of course, comes down to one thing: internal- izing Scripture. We need to get the Word inside us in order for rewriting to take place. It's something so simple and obvious that one is almost afraid to suggest it. But we have to memo- rize Scripture. Get that notebook committed to memory. Absorb those expansive circles. We're all nodding our heads right now. Memorizing Scripture is like using dental floss: Everybody thinks it's a good idea, but not many make it a habit. For a variety of reasons this classic Christian discipline is difficult to get hooked on.

For a lot of us, the words of the Bible are so vaguely familiar that they rarely inspire zealous ingestion. It's like taking the time to memorize the Declaration of Independence. Others have found the practice difficult to keep up. It gets to be routine—the more you memorize, the less it comes to mean. Many have also been turned off by Bible-quoting oddballs whose strained religiosity makes it difficult for us to relate to them comfortably on a human level.

But rewriting with the Word can be enjoyable and richly rewarding. Here are some ways I discovered, after many false starts and long stops, to memorize Scripture and like it.

## Make It Devotional

First, don't separate the work of memorizing Bible passages from your devotional life. It can be either a dry mental exercise or an edifying spiritual experience. Remember that you are internalizing the mind of God; you're getting in touch with Him. So meditate on the passage first. Savor each phrase. The use of one particular word rather than a synonym might have special significance. Try to form a mental picture of what each phrase means. Well-worn concepts like grace, faith, and peace must be coaxed into yielding up their original content. An ordinary dictionary may help you shake a concrete image loose from a vague cliché.

Try to imagine what impression this Scripture thought would give to people hearing the words for the first time. In order to better relate this idea to your own experience, you might want to write your own paraphrase of the verse.

God is continually articulating His Word; it's not something frozen on the page. Through it He maintains a present connection with you. So listen for the message He wants to communicate right now.

## Use Different Versions

Many people recommend memorizing in one literal version of the Bible. While it is less confusing to work from one translation, I can't help wallowing in what I consider pure luxury: an abundance of excellent English versions of the Scriptures. If the Hebrew and Greek really do have subtle shades of meaning that add much to the text, why not get several shots at these connotations through the efforts of different translators?

It's true that memorizing solely from a free paraphrase means you get the word more-or-less secondhand, already partly digested for you. But many dynamic translations have enough thought-for-thought equivalence to present you with a fresh, nutritious meal.

I get uptight when the pressure is on. The Amplified Bible struck a bulls-eye for me in Colossians 3:12 when it defined the patience we are to put on as that "which is tireless, long-suffering and has the power to endure whatever comes, with good temper." It helped make that virtue-objective sizzle.

The New English Bible whetted my appetite for intimate communion with Christ through its description of the two disciples from Emmaus deep in their afterglow — "Did we not feel our hearts on fire as he talked with us on the road and explained the scriptures to us?" (Luke 24:32)

## Adopt Short-Term Goals

In order not to fizzle out after a few weeks of enthusiastic effort, you need to have memory projects which can be completed in a set period of time. Short-term goals give you the feeling you're going somewhere, accomplishing something, rather than just memorizing sporadically out of the mass of Scripture.

Here's where concentrating on passages related to battle cries, identity in Christ, a counterpoint virtue, or making a last stand can be stimulating. You're filling out a definite circle of offense. Creating a "Best of Praise" collection, for example, from various vivid portrayals of God's majesty and holiness, gave me a definite, highly motivating objective in my study of the Word.

## Review

Memorized Scripture can seem like taxed income: the more that comes in, the more that slips away. In order to retain and build on what is already stored in your brain, you have to keep reviewing.

I use a two-step method. First I write down the verse I'm memorizing on a small card I carry around. Then, as more verses are added to the card over a two- or three-week period, I keep reviewing the whole group of passages. When the paper is full, and the verses memorized, I transfer them to my notebook under various headings. Periodic review of the notebook gives me an organized, functional grasp of my ever-expanding circles of offense.

## Use What You Memorize

The best way to get hooked on memorizing Scripture is to use it in daily life and experience its potent influence. It's pretty hard to become fluent in a foreign language if you are only exposed to it once a week in a classroom. But if you can live in that culture, using that language and speaking it frequently, it's much more efficiently absorbed.

So constantly expand the domain of Scripture—beyond church or Bible study group. Use it in the shopping mall, office, freeway. Make your circles work for you.

I remember the day I was impressed by the value of having a portable Word. I was riding in the subway, surrounded by smirking ads, salacious posters, a crowd of elbows, blank faces pressed close. The whole monolithic gloom of the city started weighing me down. But then in the midst of this grey desert of slick vices and squalid air I remembered that "the voice of the Lord shakes the wilderness," that His words are pure as "silver refined in a crucible" and that God wanted His people freed from Egypt so they could celebrate a feast with Him in the wilderness.

As more of the Word flickered through my mind I realized that even in a cheerless subway you can "taste and see that the Lord is good." Finding yourself banqueting away in the crush of glum commuters is the kind of experience that develops a permanent thirst for more of this effectual Word of God.

Remember to always come full circle. You started the process of memorizing in the context of the devotional life. Make the practice devotional too. In all the Scripture which helps you replace old habits with new virtues, learn to see the face of God.

## The Reason for Seeing

On January 9, 1957, John Howard Griffin stepped out of his workshop into the sunshine and received the greatest shock of his life: "Everything looked like red sand in front of my eyes." The man had suddenly regained his sight.

Griffin had suffered a concussion during World War II when a B-24 loaded with bombs exploded nearby, and he'd gradually become totally blind. But now, somehow, the twelve-year-old blockage of blood circulation to the optic nerve had been broken.

This man wrote a remarkable journal which documents his emotional, mental, and spiritual journey from blindness to sight. Learning to focus his eyes again took time. His new sensations were so intense that he had to be sedated on occassion. After a few days he cloistered himself at Mount Carmel Seminary in order to reduce all this overwhelming new data to a manageable level.

Griffin had never seen his wife or his two small children. Two-year-old Susan was the first one to rush up to a sighted Daddy. "I concentrated beyond my strength and saw all the radiant wisdom of her . . . face looking up at me. . . . That first clear view of my daughter [was] like looking at the sun—blinding me to everything else. It was there in front of my face during the next dim hours."

Griffin feared going to sleep. Would he wake up blind again? And yet there was comfort in the dark. He wrote of being brought to a cell for the night by a priest. "When he turned off the light, I felt as though a burden were lifted from me. I felt safe, at home in the dark. . . . All day the light has had this exhausting effect, and now, with it off, things relax back to some semblance of normalcy."

Each day brought challenges as he slowly came to terms with his new ability: "Certainly this adjustment is more difficult than the one to blindness, filled with a thousand clumsinesses, frustrations and complexities never dreamed of. I cannot remember that I can see."

This very sensitive, reflective man sometimes found himself feeling around in the dark for the meaning of sight. It was supposed to completely change his life, but he felt something was missing. Then one Sunday he wrote: "I have waited for the joys of sight, those joys which all have told me I should feel, and which I have felt in smaller measure than expected. But this morning they have come to me; for this morning I picked up the office and began reading those marvelous texts. . . . And in that recitation there was the intense, breaking-through of joy for which sight served as the instrument."

In his devotional reading of praises to God, Griffin discovered "the soul's nourishment, the soul's normalcy" and found himself "sinking beyond words to their innermost meaning." Finally seeing made ultimate sense. In the "clear black type of the office" this man "found full reason and justification for seeing again."

As each of us struggles out of whatever darkness our habits have enshrouded us in, we go through some of the same adjustments which Griffin wrote about. We've grown accustomed to living in the dark; trying to focus on a particular virtue takes some getting used to. We stumble about inexplicably in the light, even though we know full well it's much better than what we're turning away from.

People tell us we should be rejoicing, and we do. Still, something's missing in our pursuit of hidden treasure. It can, in fact, get quite wearying, like a great weight laid on us.

But then we finally catch a glimpse of what our virtue expresses, what its light shines on ultimately. Our looking is helping us see the face of our Lord. We can experience something of what it's like to be God; we can get inside Him.

That's when our pursuit brings the greatest joy. All that we do is for a relationship, a knowing. That's what it all means. Pursuing the good life becomes an instrument, and God's glory is the painting on which we add our brush strokes.